Few people actually have a blueprint f[...] even their days. They just let life happe[...] [...] wonder why success is so hard to find. In Dan's new book, *Positioning for Breakthrough*, he not only will walk you through the steps to help you see your future but also will show you how to build it. *Positioning for Breakthrough* should be your next read on the way to your very own breakthrough!

—PASTOR GARY KEESEE
FOUNDING PASTOR, FAITH LIFE CHURCH
PRESIDENT AND FOUNDER, FORWARD FINANCIAL GROUP

This servant of God has developed tremendous abilities to administrate and govern what God has put in his hands, and I am grateful that he wants to share these biblical principles that have made him so successful with the world. There are proven nuggets of wisdom, godly counsel, and biblical direction being offered to whoever wants more out of life. Read it several times, take notes, and put into action the insights that Pastor Dan is sowing into your life, and you will see progress.

—PASTOR MIKE BLACK
FOUNDER AND DIRECTOR, MIKE BLACK MINISTRIES

James tells us it isn't enough to be hearers; we must be doers as well. The great thing about this book is that you won't be content merely to read it. Dan wants to prepare us to take action so when opportunities for breakthrough come, we will be ready.

—PASTOR GREG SURRATT
FOUNDING PASTOR, SEACOAST CHURCH

PRESIDENT AND COFOUNDER, ASSOCIATION OF RELATED CHURCHES (ARC)

For years I have watched Dan take the ordinary and make it great. He is a man with more than just vision; he is a man with a plan. You will be encouraged as he unpacks God's Word on this subject and shares his own journey of breakthroughs. This is a message that is so needed and can help the church prepare for the next great season ahead.

—MICHAEL W. SMITH
DIRECTOR OF GLOBAL NETWORKS FOR ARC

Dan Stallbaum has been a friend for many years, and I can attest that the words written here are more than just great advice; it is honestly how Dan leads himself and his family. Within minutes this book had me challenged and encouraged to shift some things in my life so that I could be in a better position for my own break-through. This is a must-read!

—PASTOR JOSH MAUNEY
SENIOR PASTOR, NEWSOUND CHURCH
DIRECTOR OF CHURCH PLANTING FOR ARC

Positioning for Breakthrough is another example of Pastor Dan Stallbaum "keeping it real." He candidly shares his own personal successes and weaknesses and applies the Scriptures in such a way that they will immediately become applicable to your daily situations and struggles. Expect breakthrough and a vision for your future as you realize that God really does have a plan for your victory.

—DAVID M. WHITLEY, MD

Pastor Dan is truly an inspiration, a courageous and knowledgeable role model to people of all ages who are looking to change the world, even if it is one small truth at a time. His many testimonies leading to breakthrough show us that God always has a strategy to take us to the next level in our lives.

—GRADY L. GOOLSBY, DC

I have known Pastor Dan for many years. He is anointed in demonstrating practical applications of God's Word, and he illustrates this in his book *Positioning for Breakthrough*. Above all, he reminds us not only to seek out godly principles, but to seek out the principal One.

—THOMAS S. HOLT, MD

For a season I was privileged to personally serve with Pastor Dan and observe as he and our pastoral team worked diligently to position East Coast Christian Center to successfully impact the community with the Good News. This book embodies what he has learned and put into action. Pastor Dan presents a refined biblical approach to positioning oneself to reside in God's best for your life.

—REV. WILLIE W. COOPER II
COLONEL, US AIR FORCE (RET.)

My wife, Jayne, and I were privileged and blessed to be in attendance at East Coast Christian Center during Pastor Dan's six-part teaching on *Positioning for Breakthrough*. We were excited to learn that Pastor Dan had decided to present the biblical and practical benefits of these teachings in book form. Pastor Dan has written with feeling and expressed biblical truths that will change the readers' lives! We highly recommend this book as a must read!

—BILL AND JAYNE CONDON
PRESIDENT/CEO AND SECRETARY/TREASURER
OF ASSOCIATION SERVICES OF AMERICAN, INC.

As a twenty-eight-year US Air Force veteran with a number of years in space launch, I am fully aware of the importance of positioning. Proper positioning is the key to mission success. In this book Pastor Dan provides some practical ways believers can position themselves for breakthrough when facing the challenging circumstances in today's world.

—ANDRE LOVETT
COLONEL, US AIR FORCE (RET.)

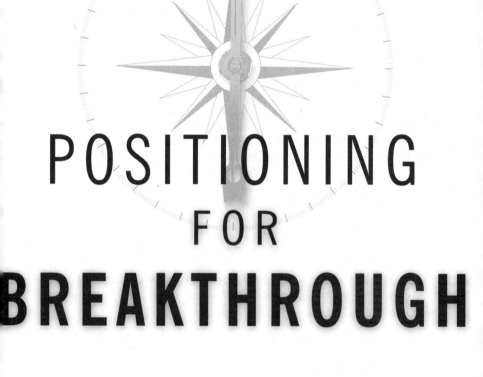

POSITIONING
FOR
BREAKTHROUGH

God's Plan for Your Victory

Dan Stallbaum
with Gisele Altman

To the one who best knows my heart and the true intent behind this book—and who has experienced and witnessed firsthand the process repeatedly work for years. I dedicate this book to my wonderful wife, Carolyn, who has been by my side for every venture and in every breakthrough for more than forty years. Thank you. I love you with all my heart, and I thank God every day for the gift of you!

ARE YOU READY FOR YOUR PERSONAL BREAKTHROUGH?

FEELING STUCK or in need of a breakthrough in any area of your life? To help you see where you can grow and experience a breakthrough, take this brief Breakthrough Assessment and see how you score. This questionnaire should take less than 5 minutes to complete.

For each of the seven categories below, respond to the statements listed down the left-hand column by placing a number from 1-5 in each box as follows:

1 - Strongly Disagree   2 - Disagree   3 - Neither Agree nor Disagree   4 - Agree   5 - Strongly Agree

	Personal	Spiritual	Professional	Financial	Mental	Physical	Emotional	**Total**
I continually breakthrough.								
I surrender to God's will and direction.								
I am obedient and responsive to God.								
I have fulfilled dreams and desires.								
I am prepared to act on a breakthrough, when it presents itself.								
Total								

Add the total number value in each of the five rows and write it in the blank space in the far-right column. Also add the total number value in each of the seven columns. Circle the lowest three number values in both the right and bottom cells. As you read the book, keep these areas in mind as you will want to focus your prayer and attention on them. It is our prayer that these weak areas will be strengthened and conquered so you can reach your breakthrough.

CONTENTS

FOREWORD

I MET DAN STALLBAUM in the 1980s at a church in Colorado. He became a staff member at his current church in Merritt Island, Florida, and rose to become the pastor in a very hard situation. I spoke there many times over two decades, and I was amazed to see how the church not only survived but thrived. This didn't happen accidentally. I was especially impressed with the way Dan and his staff worked together to advance God's kingdom and not their own. That's rare today.

Now, decades later, they have a thriving church, reaching tens of thousands, which is testimony enough that what he is doing works. I've spent a lot of hours with Dan and have seen his love for the Lord and compassion toward others, but I'm most impressed with his ability to lead and administer. He knows what he is talking about in this book. This was a weakness in my life, and I've learned a lot from Dan and implemented it. He has blessed and enriched my life immensely. I have some of his DNA in me.

I can say without reservation that ministry is 10 percent inspiration and 90 percent perspiration. Ministry is a business, and a big ministry is big business. We need the administrative and practical business skills Dan lays out in this book. I challenge you to prayerfully read this and make adjustments. This will bless not only you but also the people the Lord wants to reach through you. Don't limit God. Reach your full potential. This book will help!

—ANDREW WOMMACK
FOUNDER, ANDREW WOMMACK MINISTRIES
AND CHARIS BIBLE COLLEGE

PREFACE

THERE ARE SEASONS IN all our lives when we need a "tune-up," and during one of those seasons, I was questioning why my life had become stagnant. I recognized that while I often grew in ministry—almost every day—at times I was still challenged to stay fresh in my relationship with Christ. I was in need of a personal breakthrough, even though I had been a Christian for more than thirty years and a pastor for most of them, and I had preached at the same amazing church for more than twenty-five.

My name is Dan Stallbaum, and my search for a breakthrough led to these questions: How do breakthroughs happen, anyway? Are they magical? Do they only happen for special people?

Then I began to seek answers.

I prayed and focused on "breaking through." I even asked people I respected what "breaking through" looked like to them. As I gathered information, my personal journey grew into a six-part sermon series. Years later, and after much encouragement from my wife, Carolyn; my family; and other pastors, I sought help to transform that sermon series into this book.

On the pages that follow is the end result of my years of research. Read on and discover how you, too, can experience breakthrough.

ACKNOWLEDGMENTS

FIRST AND FOREMOST, I thank God and my Lord and Savior, Jesus Christ, for saving my life. There would be no book, nor a Pastor Dan, if it weren't for my salvation.

Acknowledgments are difficult because they open the opportunity for inadvertently leaving someone out. If that happens, know that it is not intentional, nor does that mean your contributions were not valuable. It just means my mind was overflowing.

When I thought of turning my "Positioning for Breakthrough" sermon series into a book, I received incredible encouragement from those whom I hold most dear: my wife, Carolyn; and my children, Matthew, Jessica, Jonathan, and Daniel. Thank you for your love and support. You, individually and as a family, keep me going!

As for creating the book, I would like to thank my writing partner, Gisele Altman, for taking my nine-year-old vision and original draft and transforming them into something that everyone could understand. I appreciate you using your God-given gift of writing, as well as your tireless quest for perfection, to bring *Positioning for Breakthrough: God's Plan for Your Victory* to fruition.

On a professional and personal level, I thank Pastors David Ellis, Ray Goolsby, Bryan Moore, and Matthew Stallbaum for sharing your ideas and wisdom. As for the rest of East Coast's pastoral staff, thank you for inspiring me to move forward.

Jessica Howard, thank you for continually keeping me on schedule and helping behind the scenes in too many ways to count. I'd also like to recognize my elite, God-loving co-workers who stood behind my dream and helped me follow through. You all make it a joy to come to work.

Gary and Drenda Keesee, thank you for years of friendship and for insight during our Alaska trip in 2010. Our hours of conversation only validated that this book needed to be written. I also want to thank the Association of Related Churches and all the incredible men and women of faith we are encouraged by and get to do life with every day.

Thank you, to the skilled editors who dotted i's, crossed t's, and kept us within the guidelines.

Finally, but not least, I'd like to thank my East Coast Christian Center family and congregation for driving me to be the best pastor that I can be. I remain awed by the anointed, generous, and gifted people who make up the East Coast family. I am humbled to serve as your pastor.

INTRODUCTION

I REMEMBER LEAVING FOR church early one Sunday morning to set up for services when an elderly neighbor rolled a 1960s Cadillac DeVille out of his garage. It was pristine and had a "For Sale" sign on it. The DeVille was a two-toned pearl essence dusty rose-colored convertible with an immaculate red leather interior. The odometer showed less than sixty thousand original miles, and in 1988 he was asking only eight hundred dollars for this show-worthy car.

I pulled over, and we spoke about the car, which was beautiful. His asking price was eight hundred dollars, yet it was worth so much more. He offered to let me drive it, then tossed the keys to me. I drove it around the corner to my home and showed it to Carolyn. But, regardless of how amazing this deal was, we had just moved to Florida from Colorado, were managing a newly-established business, and had three kids in private school. By no means were we prepared to spend eight hundred dollars on an investment car. I couldn't take advantage of such a great deal. I made a decision that day that if a breakthrough deal ever presented itself again, I would be prepared.

Breakthroughs can be anything from getting a great bargain to conquering inhibiting habits, excelling at something after a plateau, or breaking a glass ceiling. Additionally, some life experiences, such as getting promoted, losing weight, quitting smoking, or buying a home, are breakthroughs. Breakthroughs are always personal—in some cases they may be greater or lesser than these examples—and should be acknowledged and celebrated.

And while achieving a breakthrough satisfies a personal goal, that achievement can have a great corporate effect. Let me explain.

Your personal breakthroughs will spill over into your relationships, your abilities on the job, and the way you manage your businesses. That is how it should be. Being positioned for breakthrough should affect all aspects of your life.

Take the history of our church. In 1985 a small group of families laid the foundation for what is now East Coast Christian Center (East Coast) in Merritt Island, Florida. By 1987, they were 120 strong and bought a 13,000-square-foot movie theater. That building served as the main sanctuary, office space, and children's church. As time progressed, the church grew and purchased neighboring buildings; then it grew again.

Now, thirty years later, we manage seventeen services a week: eleven live in-house and six online. Additionally, we broadcast live special events, including our monthly Night of Worship. In 2010 we added a monthly date night outreach geared toward enhancing relationships among couples in our congregation. On those evenings, after the Saturday services, which usually end by 7:00 p.m., we provide professional day care for kids until 10:00 p.m. while their parents enjoy date night.

> **Being positioned for breakthrough should affect all aspects of your life.**

All these services are managed among four campuses and three websites (ECCC.us, YouTube, and Facebook) and require twenty-seven full-time staff members, fifty-three part-timers, and more than 1,300 Dream Team servants (volunteers). All this is done to serve nearly 3,050 attendees each week and 12,000 viewers each month.

Art Reichle, UCLA head baseball coach for thirty years, once told me, "Practice does not make perfect; perfect practice makes perfect," and, "The harder I work, the 'luckier' I get." In other words, if you're prepared, you will always have the advantage. However, the reverse is also true: When you are not prepared, breakthroughs can come to you yet not do you any good. To fully benefit from breakthroughs, you need to be ready for them so you can take full advantage when they do come.

What would your life look like right now if you had captured the last three opportunities that passed by, or if you had responded to the door that opened for you?

> *For we are His workmanship, created in Christ Jesus for good works, which God prepared beforehand that we should walk in them.*
> —*Ephesians 2:10*

God's will is for you to walk in breakthrough—and you can. But like me, people are not always prepared. As you learn the principles in this book and practice them, you should experience more breakthroughs in your life. In the upcoming chapters, we will explore different areas that will impact every area of your life.

In God's economy, East Coast's continued growth directly correlated with how we positioned ourselves for more from the very beginning. One of the reasons God blessed our church with more is that we sought to properly manage most every breakthrough, no matter how small. We tried to prepare for a breakthrough by having our house in financial and administrative order. This made room for new breakthroughs, and we were

> To fully benefit from breakthroughs, you need to be ready for them so you can take full advantage when they do come.

able to respond to any increases we received.

In my personal life, while I still do my best, in reality, life has not always worked out for me to be prepared for every breakthrough. As I get older, however, I am growing into the principle that breakthrough can only be fully reaped by those who are prepared. I have modified Art's saying to fit my beliefs: "The harder and the smarter I work, the more breakthroughs I will capture."

We need to know the source of our breakthroughs.

Notably, we need to know the source of our breakthroughs. All our efforts are in vain if we don't faithfully depend on the "Lord of the Breakthrough," as David did in 2 Samuel:

> *So David inquired of the LORD, saying, "Shall I go up against the Philistines? Will You deliver them into my hand?" And the LORD said to David, "Go up, for I will doubtless deliver the Philistines into your hand." So David went to Baal Perazim, and David defeated them there; and he said, "The LORD has broken through my enemies before me, like a breakthrough of water." Therefore he called the name of that place Baal Perazim.*
> —*2 Samuel 5:19–20*

Translated, Baal Perazim means "Lord of the Breakthrough." The Bible tells us that God has plans for us—plans to prosper us:

> *For I know the thoughts that I think toward you, says the LORD, thoughts of peace and not of evil, to give you a future and a hope.*

—*Jeremiah 29:11*

The Bible also says He will not stop training us up:

...being confident of this very thing, that He who has begun a good work in you will complete it until the day of Jesus Christ.

—*Philippians 1:6*

How will God trust you with the next plan if you don't properly see your current one through? God put it on my heart to *"enlarge the place of [my] tent"* (Isaiah 54:2) by turning a six-part sermon into a book. What you are now reading is my fulfillment of that plan.

As you continue reading, know that the Bible is the infallible, inerrant Word of God, and the final authority in all matters of faith and conduct (2 Timothy 3:15-17, 1 Peter 2:22). For this reason, this book is based on biblical teachings, along with my life experiences. As Christians, we need to understand that the Bible interprets the Bible. That means that the Bible clarifies itself by giving verses and principles that explain other verses and principles. In other words, if you read something in the Bible that isn't immediately clear, you will eventually find that same principle somewhere else in the Bible which will explain it in a way that's understandable to you. And while there are various translations of the Bible, for this book, I mostly used The New King James Version as my primary source for quoted Scriptures; with an occasional secondary source. (Secondary sources will be noted as such.)

The Bible interprets the Bible.

In the following pages is information that will help you prepare to receive God's best for you. God loves you too much to leave you where you are; He wants to elevate you to your full purpose and potential. Your purpose in life is to glorify Him:

> *Everyone who is called by My name, whom I have created for My glory; I have formed him, yes, I have made him.*
> —*Isaiah 43:7*

Glorifying Him requires continued growth as a Christian. And we grow as Christians "*from glory to glory*" (2 Corinthians 3:18), from breakthrough to breakthrough.

God has a breakthrough for you. Now is the time to position yourself for it. Read on and let Him speak to you and prepare you for when it comes.

CHAPTER 1

PROPER ADMINISTRATION: THE MISSING LINK

IN 2010 MY WIFE, Carolyn, and I went on a trip with our dear friends Gary and Drenda Keesee. Gary had approached us and asked, "Why don't we go to Alaska? We'll rent an RV and spend eight or nine days fishing."

I was all for that. I like to fish. No, I love to fish. Gary also loves to fish, and since we both love ministry, I knew that this had the makings of a great trip. Arrangements were made, and weeks later we met in Fairbanks, Alaska, for our trip.

As the four of us waited to be picked up and taken to our RV, I received a call from one of our executive pastors concerning some important changes that East Coast Christian Center was making. The management team had been analyzing every fiscal area, from lawn services to phone carriers to banking costs, as well as reviewing each department and asking God, "Is this the best we can do?"

Since we were making a significant decision about our banking, that call required my immediate attention. I relayed my decision to the caller and asked him to initiate our changes. Gary, overhearing the conversation, asked me what East Coast was doing. I told him that as a church we were positioning ourselves for increase and breakthrough, which meant getting our "house in order." He and I began to discuss the specifics and what it meant for the church, and as the conversation progressed, things began to get really exciting.

Our conversation continued throughout the 200-mile RV journey to our fishing spot; all the while Gary was feverishly taking notes.

Gary then asked, "How do you do what you do?"

Puzzled, I asked him what he meant.

"Don't take this wrong, but what you are doing at your church is impossible. How do you do it?"

I still wasn't sure what he meant, so I was unable to respond to his question. I asked him to elaborate.

"Look, Dan," he said, "you have an 8:30 service, and you fill up the house. At the end of the service everyone leaves, and fifteen minutes later your six hundred–person sanctuary is full for the 10:00 service. And at the end of that service, it empties and fills up again within fifteen minutes for the 11:30 service. Not only do you fill the main building but also the two-hundred person video venue next door. No one else in the country allows only fifteen minutes for an entire sanctuary of people to leave and then fills it again within that same time frame. Most churches refuse to have three Sunday morning services for that reason. You are doing the impossible. How do you do it?"

I pondered Gary's observation. "I don't know if I even want to know," I said. "I guess I was too dumb to think that we couldn't. I don't know."

As I thought about it more, I realized the "impossibility" of our Sunday mornings didn't end there. We have our children's ministry, which we call "Children's Church," in a separate building, which could cause even more time issues because people have to cross the large parking lot to drop off their children and then walk back to the sanctuary for service. The parking lot is full during each service and will not fit the people who are coming to the next one. Yet somehow it empties and fills back up within fifteen minutes. Thank you, Jesus.

Please understand, I acknowledge that God enables us to do anything we do, even if it seems impossible, and He deserves all the glory. But—and this is a big but—since God has given us a large amount of land and several buildings, we need to be able to utilize them practically and properly. I then realized that there was one thing that made this all work: proper administration. We were correctly administrating the things we had been given.

Four Synonyms for Administration

There aren't many sermons written on the topic of administration. Why? Because it sounds boring. Some readers want to set this book down right now and could be thinking, "How boring can we get?" Let me stop you right there. I felt the same way before I began to dig into the Word and see how important this topic truly is. What I found was a Bible full of examples of and instructions on how to properly administrate what God has given you. There is so much power released when you begin to administrate your life in a godly, biblical way. To help you clearly understand what "administrating your life" looks like, I share four synonyms for administrate.

> The Bible is full of examples of and instructions on how to properly administrate what God has given you.

1. Manage. The first synonym is *manage*. I am not referring to being the type of manager who sits in his office and does nothing except boss everyone else around. Most of us have dealt with that type of manager at one time or another. Rather, I'm talking about the type of manager who enables his or her team members to get the job done and to do it well. A great manager forms a cohesive team, gets the team members on the same page to understand and pursue the same vision while doing the right job at the right time. I am talking about the good, godly, and talented manager.

2. Direct. Another synonym for *administrate* is *direct*. Movie directors are involved in every aspect of the film. They direct the lighting, the cinematography, the actors, the story, and everything else. They are the ones pulling it all together. Each of the individual parts wouldn't accomplish anything if they didn't have a director. A good director, or administrator, pulls not only his people but all the other key elements together to achieve a desired outcome.

3. Govern. The third synonym is *govern*. This is not a negative term when it refers to God's type of government. I don't know about you, but my life dramatically transformed when the government of God came in. My life beforehand was disgustingly broken. I'm not proud of it, but back in the day I sold drugs and made tens of thousands of dollars doing so. Yet I never had any money. I never had anything, for that matter, because I didn't know how to govern my life. In all aspects my life was a broken mess because I didn't have the government of God.

The Bible says in Isaiah:

> *And the government will be upon His shoulder. And His name will be called Wonderful Counselor, Mighty God, Everlasting Father, Prince of Peace.*
> —Isaiah 9:6

That is the type of government I am talking about.

4. Steward. The fourth synonym for *administrate*, *steward*, is a biblical word that we normally associate with finances; however, it applies to much more. Stewardship means taking charge of things given to you by God and responsibly managing those resources in a good, godly, and powerful way. When we properly administrate what He has given us, we become good stewards.

These four terms—manage, direct, govern, and steward—all describe *administrate* in a surrogate form, meaning you are responsible for maintaining what has been given to you. The Word of God has so much to say about administration. I will share examples, and when you study them for yourself, you will find that most of the great victories in the Bible came on the heels of proper administration. Similarly, God wants to move us. God wants to position us so we can walk in the breakthroughs that He has planned for our lives (Jeremiah 29:11).

The Strategy

Walking in these breakthroughs requires you to assess where you are and take action.

Assess Where You Are

As a church body, in 2009—the year we began positioning for our breakthroughs—East Coast grew nearly 20-percent. Financially, the year before, we had grown 6-percent. So we weren't reassessing ourselves because we had to in order to make it; we were already doing well and continually expanding. Rather, we made those changes because God wanted us to be better stewards of what we had. We inherently wanted to do a more excellent job with what we had been given.

We first reviewed our office phone system and decided to

switch to a different company. That saved us more than $200 each month. We then changed our cell phone provider, which saved us another $100 each month.

Then one day as I was walking into the office, our lawn service provider stopped me. He told me that since we had planted new grass by one of our buildings, he was going to have to charge us more to maintain it. I asked him to submit a bid, and we would let him know. He walked away and I thought, "You know, I don't have any idea what we are paying him to maintain our lawn. Not a clue."

Before I became a pastor, I had a lawn and landscaping business for several years, so I sat at my desk and spent fifteen minutes writing a bid that I thought was appropriate for our campus. I walked down the property, examined the square footage, and determined exactly how much property we had. I then calculated what it would take to keep it mowed and trimmed. Because of my previous experience in the lawn care and landscaping business, I felt extremely confident of my calculations. My bid amount was $350 a month. I went to one of our executive pastors and asked what we were paying for lawn service.

"Five hundred dollars," he said.

"Put the lawn maintenance position out for bids," I told him.

Sure enough, we got a bid for $325 from a very reputable person, who also attended our church. I told him we would pay him $350, and we gave him the job. His bid was cheaper than our original provider even before he raised his rates. That change was now saving us more than $150 a month.

If you do the math, between the office phones, cell phone provider, and lawn service, we were saving $5,400 a year. That's a $5,400 increase toward God's kingdom just by making small adjustments to how we managed what we already had.

Now let's go back to that significant decision I made while vacationing with the Keesees in Alaska. East Coast had been banking with the same bank for more than twelve years. Normally when something works for you, you stick with it. However, I decided we couldn't do that anymore because God had put a transition on my heart. I asked our financial director for a printout of every banking expense we were being charged. I wanted to know how much it cost to bank with that company. Then I collected the same information from other banks to compare fee structures. One bank sent a proposal that at a minimum would save us more than $10,000 a year. Without question we changed banks.

Whether saving $100 a month or $10,000 a year, paying attention to the large and small details is the kind of stuff you need to do to position yourself for breakthrough. We took the time to dig below the surface and go deeper, and it all paid off.

Please note, however, that leaving a business partnership likely will not be easy, especially when a kinship has formed. In some instances the personal attention and efforts of the personnel leave us with a sense of loyalty toward that business. When deciding to depart from such a relationship, you will need to discern what is best for you and if the financial difference is worth the change. Also, in those cases where it is worth it, where the amount is substantial enough, you might consider giving that business an opportunity to closely match the better offers. Either way, you will need to pray and ask God for wisdom and guidance when deciding between these relationships and what's best for your business.

Now remember, in 2008 we grew financially by 6 percent, yet we still researched and administrated all those changes by the summer of 2009. By the last quarter of 2009 we had grown financially by 20 percent. All our efforts were being validated. And astoundingly, we saw a 50 percent increase in attendance from 2009, when we had 87,241 attendees, to 2016, when 131,020 people attended. I firmly believe that our growth was directly correlated with our administration of what we had—even from the beginning.

If you start by assessing where you are and then making changes—no matter how small—to become a better steward of what you have, you will see breakthrough and be given more. If God can get the importance of this message of proper administration into your life, I promise your life will dramatically change.

For instance, if you want to grow in your knowledge of God, make a change. Join a Bible study or start a Bible study reading plan. No matter what steps you take, God will honor your efforts. And this advice works the same way emotionally, financially, and relationally (e.g., in marriage, budgeting, and work relationships).

There's a saying, "Insanity is doing the same thing over and over again and expecting different results."[1] While often incorrectly attributed to Albert Einstein, the point made is that it is unwise to repeat actions that are ineffective. These actions will keep you stuck and waste how you manage your time. Instead, make a change.

Our radio show, *Morning Breath*, for example, gives the listeners the opportunity to read a chapter of the Bible and listen to a discussion on the chapter. If you did that, you would be participating in a daily devotional. And *Morning Breath* was born because decades ago I began reading a chapter a day. I took a step.

It's Time to Move

We've all heard of people who have received an inheritance and within a few years don't have any of the money left. According to the National Endowment for Financial Education, 70 percent of all million-dollar lottery winners are in debt three years later.[2] Why? Because they don't know how to manage their money. The lottery makes an easy target of people who dream of having something big but don't know how to administrate it when they get it. When they finally do get it, it disappears in a short time because they do not have the skills to be a good steward of what they have received.

I have seen people receive successful businesses, both from family or from an investment, and within a short time the business is bankrupt. What happened? What changed? I believe it's an administration problem.

Let's step out of the business/financial realm for a minute and talk about marriage, where this principle also applies. I believe many marriages fail not because of a lack of love but because of a lack of administration. **If you do not manage your life, someone or something else will.** Properly administrating a marriage involves taking the time to learn about each other, adjusting one's life to fit into the other's life, and positioning oneself to be who he or she needs to be for the other person.

A simple illustration would be the words "I love you." What does that mean to you? More importantly, what does that mean to your spouse? In our relationship I learned early on that Carolyn and I spoke different love languages. Because of our vastly different upbringings, Carolyn's love needs were addressed through acts of service. For instance, when I clean the garage, that act of service makes Carolyn feel truly loved. My love needs were more tactile; I required a loving touch or verbal affirmation to truly feel loved.

To learn each other's love languages, we had to administrate our marriage by spending time learning the other's definition of *love*. Then we made changes to improve our marriage by giving the love that our spouse needed, rather than the love we *thought* the other needed. That alleviated the frustration that comes from giving the love we need instead of the love the *other person needs.*

Would you like to be in a position to succeed in every area of your life? You already are. God has given you *"all things that pertain to life and godliness."*

> His divine power has given to us all things that pertain to life and godliness, through the knowledge of Him who called us by glory and virtue.
>
> —2 Peter 1:3

By faith we receive what God has given to us by His grace. If you are not experiencing success, what would need to change? Hebrews 13:8 tells us that *"Jesus Christ is the same yesterday, today, and forever."* So most likely *you* are the one who needs to make an adjustment. Is there something you could do to move your progress along? By faith we receive what God has given to us by His grace. Many times we are waiting on God, but as in a tennis game, God has already given us what we need to be successful, and He's waiting on our return of serve. The same goes for your personal relationship with Him. James 4:8 states that when you *"draw near to God ... He will draw near to you."*

God is the initiator. He has already provided us good works before it was ordained that we should walk in them (Ephesians 2:10). When God has "served" the ball, it's up to us to hit it back. Most times in my life when I've been waiting on God, I've realized He was actually waiting on me. I'm not trying to be harsh here, but truthfully, if you do not manage your life, someone or something else will.

The Parable of the Talents

> For the kingdom of heaven is like a man traveling to a far country, who called his own servants and delivered his

goods to them. And to one he gave five talents, to another two, and to another one, to each according to his own ability; and immediately he went on a journey. Then he who had received the five talents went and traded with them, and made another five talents. And likewise he who had received two gained two more also. But he who had received one went and dug in the ground, and hid his lord's money. After a long time the lord of those servants came and settled accounts with them.

So he who had received five talents came and brought five other talents, saying, "Lord, you delivered to me five talents; look, I have gained five more talents besides them." His lord said to him, "Well done, good and faithful servant; you were faithful over a few things, I will make you ruler over many things. Enter into the joy of your lord." He also who had received two talents came and said, "Lord, you delivered to me two talents; look, I have gained two more talents besides them." His lord said to him, "Well done, good and faithful servant; you have been faithful over a few things, I will make you ruler over many things. Enter into the joy of your lord."

Then he who had received the one talent came and said, "Lord, I knew you to be a hard man, reaping where you have not sown, and gathering where you have not scattered seed. And I was afraid, and went and hid your talent in the ground. Look, there you have what is yours."

But his lord answered and said to him, "You wicked and lazy servant, you knew that I reap where I have not sown, and gather where I have not scattered seed. So you ought to have deposited my money with the bankers, and at my coming, I would have received back my own with interest. So take the talent from him, and give it to him who has ten talents.

"For to everyone who has, more will be given, and he will have abundance; but from him who does not have, even what he has will be taken away."
—Matthew 25:14–29

This Scripture conveys the parable of the talents. There is a lot of speculation over what the talents are exactly. In that time a talent was a measure of money—such as a talent of gold or of silver. However, it could also be seen in the sense of abilities or spiritual gifts. Whatever it is, this parable is meant to be seen as God giving you something that He wants you to use and multiply.

All of us have been made for a purpose.

One thing the Scripture is very clear on, however, can be found in verse 15: *"to each according to his own ability."* The master gave each servant the exact amount he was able to handle. It doesn't matter what stage of life you're in or how much money you have; you have been given everything you need from God, and it is up to you to manage it correctly.

Three people were given gifts. One was given five, another was given two, and the other was given one. The one who was given five went out and began to trade. He invested and doubled what he had been given. He resisted fear and pressure and sought the wisdom of God. In essence, he moved out in faith. He began to look at the horizon of his life and decided to do something with what he had received. The Bible says that when his master returned, he was very pleased with his servant. The same applied to the second servant, who was given two gifts. In faith he doubled what his master had given him, and his master praised him. It doesn't matter what you're given; it's what you do with it that is important.

Then there was the third servant, who didn't quite get it. He did not move forward in faith. He was afraid and did nothing with what was given him. The servant knew the master would want his money back, so he took the money and buried it in the ground. When the master returned, the servant gave him back his money untouched and unused. What did the master say to him? He said the servant was *"wicked and lazy"* (v. 26). The servant did not understand how to properly manage the assets given to him. Then the master took the servant's talent and gave it to the one who had ten.

All of us have been made for a purpose, and we have been gifted by God to accomplish that purpose. What do you love to do? What brings you joy? What energizes you? Is it serving, leading, or giving? If it's serving, consider being a room dad or mom at your child's school. If leading is more your strength, think about coaching your daughter's volleyball team. If it's giving, find a charity that touches your heart. All in all, step out in faith in that area that speaks to you, and don't leave that gift buried.

Then we reach the summary of the story:

> *For to **everyone who has, more will be given,** and he will have abundance; but from him who does not have, even what he has will be taken away.*
> *—Matthew 25:29, emphasis added*

What is the point here? What is Jesus talking about? For everyone who "has" what, will be given "more" of what? It isn't money, because if it were, anyone who had money would be getting more money. Same with skills, or gifts. That's not the way God works. What He's saying here is that to everyone who has good stewardship principles, more will be given.

Also, this is not just for people who are wealthy. Look at what this verse says:

> It doesn't matter what you're given; it's what you do with it that is important. If you are a good steward of what God has given you, then you will be entrusted with more.

He who is faithful in what is least is faithful also in much.

—Luke 16:10

Simply put, if you are a good steward of what God has given you, then you will be entrusted with more. It's a biblical principle and promise. To him who has stewardship or administration, who is positioning himself for what God wants, more will be given. But to him who has nothing and who refuses to move toward repositioning himself, even what he has will be taken away. That's a profoundly strong word.

Hebrews 11—"the Hall of Faith"

Let's look at another portion of Scripture that explains the administration concept in a more theological way. In Hebrews 11, which many call "the hall of faith," the men and women all had extraordinary faith and received their answers from God because of it.

And what more shall I say? For the time would fail me to tell of Gideon and Barak and Samson and Jephthah, also of David and Samuel and the prophets ...

—Hebrews 11:32

The next verse, 33, is key and holds the progression that I believe we have missed: *"who through faith subdued kingdoms"* (Hebrews 11:33).

Where is the kingdom of God? Think about it. It's within you. You see, there is a law of dominion on the earth. God gave the earth to the sons of men; therefore, the earth is under the dominion of mankind. However, mankind bowed his knee to the devil in the Garden of Eden. There they partook of the fruit from the Tree of the Knowledge of Good and Evil and gave up the dominion of the earth to satan (Genesis 2–3). So now, whenever Jesus is speaking of the *"god of this world,"* He is referring to satan. This is why satan could stand on the top of a very high mountain and tempt Jesus with the promise of giving Him *"all the kingdoms of the world and their glory"* (Matthew 4:8–9). The world was now all satan's because Adam and Eve lost it to him by disobeying God.

God has a law of dominion, which He doesn't revoke, and that is why Jesus, as the Son of Man, had to come and take dominion back. But here's the point: because the kingdom of God is within you, you have the power to establish dominion over satan. Nonetheless, dominion can only be established if you recognize that as a believer, you have the power and the authority to use it.

Also, be aware that it's always easier to have dominion over your own environment. Your house should be a "place of worship." It should be a place where the Word of God is held in high esteem, over which love is the banner. But when you get in your car and drive through your neighborhood, you are not driving in the dominion of God. When you go to work, you may not be in a place where the dominion of God is prevalent. We have to take territory and establish our dominion in a world that is ruled by evil. How do we do that?

Establishing dominion, or subduing kingdoms, means we replace the areas of our lives that were previously controlled by satan with ones where God exercises His kingdom—where God reigns. And we do all this by faith. Let's say we believe God to be the determining factor in our homes. We can, by faith, release the love of God and bind hate, anger, and malice and establish God's dominion in our home.

But that's not all we have to do. Let's continue with Hebrews 11:33: *"who through faith subdued kingdoms, worked righteousness, obtained promises."*

It is not enough to subdue kingdoms by faith; you have to "work righteousness" too. What does the word work mean? It means "to toil (as a task, occupation, etc.), (by implication) effect, be engaged in or with, etc.—commit, do, labor for, minister about, trade (by), work."[3] In this case, the word *work* could be substituted with *administered*, as seen in the New International Version of the same verses:

> *And what more shall I say? I do not have time to tell about Gideon, Barak, Samson and Jephthah, about David and Samuel and the prophets, who through faith conquered kingdoms, administered justice, and gained what was promised.*
>
> *—Hebrews 11:32–33, NIV*

I believe one of the reasons the body of Christ has struggled to receive all that God has promised us is that we have missed a key part. We have subdued kingdoms but forgotten about administering justice, judgment, or righteousness.

Grace-Filled Living

Before we delve any deeper into how to administer justice, we need to understand works versus grace. Many people get stuck here. If you are performing "works of righteousness" (e.g., doing good deeds, reading chapters of your Bible, donating to charity, and so on) to obtain God's approval and love or receive His salvation, that's theological legalism (biblically referred to as the Law), and it's not correct.

This type of legalism focuses on works— in a negative sense—and is defined as "the doctrine that salvation is gained through good works."[4] More plainly stated, this type of legalism defines anything we do to earn what God, by *His grace*, has *already* given us.

> Salvation is free—a gift from God that cannot be earned by works. So stop trying to earn God's love and approval.

To make it clearer, if someone gave you a new car, would you go to the bank, set up an account, and start making monthly payments on it? Of course not. Know that legalism is not part of God's plan for your life. In other words, believing that being a good person or doing good works is enough to get you into heaven is wrong thinking. Salvation is free—a gift from God that cannot be earned by works, as Ephesians tells us. So stop trying to earn God's love and approval.

> *For by grace you have been saved through faith, and that not of yourselves; it is the gift of God, not of works, lest anyone should boast.*

—*Ephesians 2:8–9*

You aren't going to get to heaven because you deserve it. You'll get there by accepting God's gift of salvation made possible only because Jesus bled and died for your sins. You cannot work for what God has provided for you by grace. Furthermore, when we do good works, we should do them as a response to God's grace, not thinking we can earn God's grace. Look how this worked in Abraham's life:

> *What then shall we say that Abraham our father has found according to the flesh? For if Abraham was justified by works, he has something to boast about, but not before God. For what does the Scripture say? "Abraham believed God, and it was accounted to him for righteousness." Now to him who works, the wages are not counted as grace but as debt. But to him who does not work but believes on Him who justifies the ungodly, his faith is accounted for righteousness.*
> —*Romans 4:1–5*

Circumcision did nothing to earn God's approval for Abraham. It was his faith. Look at what Titus says:

> *But when the kindness and the love of God our Savior toward man appeared, not by works of righteousness which we have done, but according to His mercy He saved us.*
> —*Titus 3:4–5*

Salvation is received by faith and faith only. (For instructions on how to receive God's salvation, see Chapter 2.)

I invite you to embark on a journey of learning how to receive the promises of God—such as provision, healing, peace, and restoration—that are given to us by grace and received by faith.

Administering Justice

Now that you have a brief explanation of Law versus grace, let's focus on administering justice. Recall that Hebrews 11 shows us that we need to go beyond "conquering kingdoms" to be successful in preparation of receiving all God has for us.

> *And what more shall I say? I do not have time to tell about Gideon, Barak, Samson and Jephthah, about David and Samuel and the prophets, who through faith conquered kingdoms, **administered justice**, and gained what was promised.*
> *—Hebrews 11:32–33, NIV, emphasis added*

In 2 Samuel we find a perfect example of what administering justice looks like from a biblical perspective. Chapter 8 tells a story of King David, probably the most famous king in the Bible. This is what verse 13 says:

> *And David made himself a name when he returned from killing eighteen thousand Syrians in the Valley of Salt.*
> *—2 Samuel 8:13*

This is one of David's most successful military victories. He fought the Syrians in the valley of the Dead Sea and killed 18,000. As we think back to the children of Israel, there are dozens of biblical stories of the Israelites fighting the Philistines. But you

don't find them fighting the Syrians dozens of times. Why not?
Let's read on:

> *He also put garrisons in Edom; throughout all Edom*
> *he put garrisons, and all the Edomites became David's*
> *servants. And the LORD preserved David wherever he*
> *went. So David reigned over all Israel; and David admin-*
> *istered judgment and justice to all his people.*
> —2 Samuel 8:14–15

Here we see an example of how properly administrating judgment and justice can change the outcome of a situation. Now, most
people consider the word *judgment* a negative term, when in fact
judgment means "to decide." On any given day, we are faced with
multiple decisions and must judge when deciding what to do. Many
of our decisions are as basic as judging right from wrong.

David won a great battle, but if he had not practiced administration to keep the Syrians from retaliating, the sons of the men
who were killed would have returned in the future to seek revenge
on David. But because he established garrisons (large groups of
soldiers), he stopped the people from rising up. Throughout the
country he made them his servants, and because of administration
the victory remained his. This was the major difference between
Israel fighting the Philistines and David fighting the Syrians.
Proper administration was key for not having to fight the Syrians
over and over again.

Ponder This

Do you know someone who has fought the same battle over
and over again? They fight it, beat it—yet only temporarily—then

end up fighting it again at some later time. Why can't they achieve a complete victory? To be successful, the process outlined in Hebrews 11 needs to be followed. By faith you conquer kingdoms; then you administer righteousness, and only then do you receive the promise. It is administration that makes the difference.

I challenge you to look at the battles in your life that you repeatedly fight. Ask God to give you wisdom on what you need to do differently so you will finally conquer them, rather than keep fighting them, over and over, in the future. If you win a battle but don't change anything in your life, you will never win the war. Nor will you see different, positive results.

Finally, without performing proper administration of your life, you will never receive the promises and the freedom God has in store for you. Are you ready for a real change in your life? Do you want to be victorious? Ask God to help you properly administrate your life, your blessings, and your gifts.

Prayer

Heavenly Father, thank You for all of my blessings, gifts, and assets. Lord, I ask for wisdom to properly administrate what You have already given me. Father, I ask You to show me how to make changes that better benefit Your kingdom. I ask for Your help to conquer my weaknesses so I no longer have to fight the same battles over and over. Lord, I want positive results and changes in my life. I want to be victorious and prepared for when my breakthrough comes. In Jesus's name I pray this. Amen!

CHAPTER 2

SUBDUING AND EXPANDING KINGDOMS

WE LEARNED IN CHAPTER 1, we are here, by faith, to subdue kingdoms, and the greatest step we can take toward positioning ourselves for that is to step into Christ and make Him the center of our lives. We need to have a living, thriving relationship with God through His Son, Jesus Christ, and ask Him to be Lord of our lives. It isn't enough to simply believe that Jesus, or God exists, because James 2:19 says, *"Even the demons believe—and tremble!"* We need to do more. We have to give our hearts and lives over to Him. We have to get off the throne of our hearts and put God first in our lives.

Do you know Him? Is He part of your life? Have you asked Jesus to come live in your heart, be your Lord, King, and God? If you haven't done so, I want to give you that opportunity right now. Below is a sample prayer. If you recite this prayer and believe what you are speaking, in your heart, it will guarantee your salvation and righteousness and promise an eternity with God.

Father God, I thank You for loving me so much that You sent Jesus to die on the cross for me. I am sorry for my sins; please forgive me. I believe Jesus rose from the dead and is now with You in heaven. Jesus, come live in my heart and be my Lord and Savior. I am yours. I pray this in Jesus's holy name. Amen.

If you recited that prayer, congratulations, and welcome to the kingdom of God.

Subduing Kingdoms by Faith

Reciting the sinner's prayer and believing it in your heart are the first steps toward positioning yourself for breakthrough. By asking Jesus to be your Lord and Savior, you subdue kingdoms by faith. When you give your heart and life to Christ, your life is no longer part of someone else's kingdom; your life is now in God's kingdom.

By being part of God's kingdom, you can subdue kingdoms on earth. Subduing kingdoms entails taking the gospel outside the four walls of the church and expanding the kingdom of God. We expand the kingdom not only by sharing Christ with others but also through prayer and believing God's promises. God answers prayers when we pray for things that are in His will. The Lord's Prayer makes this clear:

> Subduing kingdoms entails taking the gospel outside the four walls of the church and expanding the kingdom of God.

Your kingdom come. Your will be done on earth as it is in heaven.
> —*Matthew 6:10*

When we pray these words, we are exercising our dominion and believing in faith for what God has promised us. We are thereby subduing a kingdom.

Have you ever struggled with poverty or experienced a time when finances were tight? Did you ever pray that God would bless you and that your financial situation would improve? If so, that act of faith is subduing a kingdom. You are taking authority, in the name of Jesus, and believing by faith that you will receive what God has provided for you by grace. Praying in faith establishes the dominion of God on the earth, and this is how we are called to pray every time we pray.

But with this authority comes responsibility. Remember, it is crucial that we follow the process of Hebrews 11:33 by first administrating our lives, working righteousness, and then obtaining the promises God has for us. Often we pray and God answers our prayers, but it is our responsibility to administrate the answered prayers properly. We may pray for healing, and then sickness and poverty leave. That's an answer to prayer. But five weeks later they're back and we're fighting them again. Why? It is most likely because our lifestyle didn't change—we didn't properly administrate the answered prayer.

I can relay this first hand as I used to be a smoker, and I know how difficult it is to stop smoking. But if you pray and ask God to heal your lungs, yet you continue to smoke, you are not administrating your life properly. Smoking will continue to damage your lungs.

Whatever the situation, it is not enough to pray and ask God to heal your body. If you don't make a lifestyle change, you will be praying that same prayer for the rest of your life. Instead, God wants you to pray that prayer and then do something about it—work righteousness, administrate justice, and obtain the promise (Hebrews 11:33).

> Praying in faith establishes the dominion of God on the earth, and this is how we are called to pray every time we pray.

Directing Your Increase

When I was twenty, I moved from Florida to Colorado, and a friend from high school followed me there. He applied for a job at the local fire department, got hired, and at the time of this printing, has been there 30 years. But while we were in high school, his older brother, upon returning from Vietnam, bought property in Missouri. Soon the rest of the family followed his brother's lead and also bought property in Missouri. All the properties connected and totaled one hundred acres. My friend owned ten acres.

Throughout high school, and even after he became a fireman in Colorado, it was my friend's responsibility to take care of and administrate those hundred acres. Every three years he had to mow it. There were large oak trees on the property that he needed a chainsaw to take down before he could mow. He spent thousands of dollars maintaining this land.

Today his family has one hundred acres in the middle of Missouri with nothing growing on it. If thirty-four years ago, when they purchased the land, they had planted pine trees, they would have been able to reap at least two or three paper mills' worth of harvests from the property by now. That's not to mention, my friend wouldn't have had to fight the large oak trees.

Increasing is not just *receiving* more. How you administrate what you already have is what determines your increase. You have to know how to expand your kingdom.

After the prayer of Jabez, God granted Jabez his request to expand his territory:

And Jabez called on the God of Israel saying, "Oh, that You would bless me indeed, and enlarge my territory, that

*Your hand would be with me, and that You would keep me
from evil, that I may not cause pain!" So God granted him
what he requested.*

—*1 Chronicles 4:10*

While these were all good things to pray for, sometimes
answered prayers don't make your life easier, particularly in the
beginning. However, if you properly administrate these blessings,
they become hugely rewarding.

I found this especially true when God literally enlarged my
territory years ago. As I drove home one day, I saw a sign advertising two vacant lots for sale: one for $35,000 and the other for
$45,000. I tried to get onto the properties to see what they looked
like, but they were so overgrown with trees and brush that I
couldn't get through without a chainsaw or a machete. The For Sale
sign showed the outline of the two lots. One of them appeared to
have a canal behind it, while the other didn't appear to be on the
water. Something about the sign didn't look right to me. It seemed
as if the pictures of the lots had been transposed on the sign.

So I went home, changed clothes, grabbed a chainsaw, hopped
in my boat, and followed the canal to the two lots. I beached my
boat at the back of the property, and using my chainsaw, I sawed
my way through to the sign out front. Sure enough, there was a
canal behind both of the lots. The sign was in error. And while the
seller and real estate agent knew that the lots were waterfront, the
error in the sign, along with their tremendously overgrown condi-
tion, deterred potential buyers. I immediately put an offer on one
of the properties, less than what the seller was asking, and ended
up buying the $35,000 waterfront lot for $32,500.

When I bought the lot, I still hadn't reached my end goal. I
was far from being finished. I went in with chainsaws and spent

days cutting everything down. After clearing the land, we built our home. But this involved designing the home, prepping the land, approving plans and blueprints, having foundations poured, and adding electricity, water, and sewer. We also needed to obtain permits and pass inspections. Overall, the entire process—from buying the land to building the home—took eighteen months. See, even after we had received our breakthrough, we had to administrate it properly.

We lived in that home for seven years and invested $160,000 in it. Then, in addition to being initially blessed with the property, a financial harvest came our way seven years later, when we sold the lot and house for $625,000.

This is further evidence that what you do with the things God has given you is what determines your increase in life. I didn't receive an immediate increase when I bought the property. Instead, initially I ended up with more work.

When God gives us something, often it is in raw form and needs a lot of work. But if you do the work, you will see the fruit of that work in your life.

Joseph's Gift of Administration

As you can see, how we administrate our lives is important. One of the best biblical examples of administration is the story of Joseph, one of Jacob's twelve sons and his favorite. Jacob showed this by giving Joseph a coat of many colors. This open display of favoritism made his brothers incredibly jealous. Additionally, because of his young age, Joseph was not too sharp on how he handled the favoritism and completely mismanaged his situation. And it didn't stop there.

At some point Joseph had two dreams. In one, he and his

brothers were binding wheat in a field when his bundle of wheat stood upright and all the brothers' bundles stood and bowed down to it. In his second dream, eleven stars represented his brothers, while the sun and the moon represented his mother and father. In this dream, they all bowed down to him (Genesis 37:9). And for naive reasons associated with inexperienced youth, Joseph boasted about his dreams to everyone.

Now Joseph wasn't very old, but his brothers were. His oldest brother, Reuben, was about thirty years older than Joseph. His boasting equated to a twelve-year-old telling his adult brother that one day he would bow down and serve him. If that were my little brother, I'd flick him in the forehead and tell him to shush up. And when Joseph shared the dream with his parents, they didn't believe him. Even though what he was relaying was from God, he didn't handle it correctly at first. The Bible tells us that this resulted in his brothers getting so angry they threw him into a pit and eventually sold him into slavery. Then they told their father that a wild beast had eaten Joseph.

Then we come to a point in the story where Joseph is standing on an auction block, completely naked, with strangers bidding on him. Do you know what the Bible says about him?

> *The LORD was with Joseph, and he was a successful man.*
> —*Genesis 39:2*

Wait a minute. Joseph is in chains, naked, and on an auction block. How is he successful? It's because of what and who was in him.

Joseph ended up being bought by a man named Potiphar. During his servitude, Joseph displayed such a God-given gift of administration and such an anointing of the presence of God in his life that Potiphar put him in charge of everything he had. Joseph took over Potiphar's house and later ended up a ruler in Egypt.

Then we learn that he wasn't in that prestigious position for long before Potiphar's wife came along and tried to seduce Joseph. He wanted nothing to do with her, so she falsely accused him of a crime and had him thrown in prison. Again, he was back in chains. But the anointing of God and the gift of administration remained so strong in his life that before long he was managing the prison.

The warden was sitting back chewing bubble gum and didn't care what was going on. If anybody had a question about the prison, they would ask Joseph—he was in charge.

When God promotes you, and you think it's about you, you're in trouble.

While Joseph was managing the prison, two men were placed in custody—the king's baker and his cupbearer. While confined, they both had dreams and shared them with Joseph. God revealed to Joseph the meaning of the cupbearer's dream:

Now within three days Pharaoh will lift up your head and restore you to your place, and you will put Pharaoh's cup in his hand according to the former manner, when you were his butler.

—Genesis 40:13

Everything was going to work out great for the cupbearer.

Then the baker asked for the interpretation of his dream. Joseph replied:

> *Within three days Pharaoh will lift off your head from you*
> *and hang you on a tree; and the birds will eat your flesh*
> *from you.*
>
> —Genesis 40:19

The Scripture reveals, things weren't going to work out as well for the baker.

Sure enough, things happened just as Joseph's interpretations of the dreams from God indicated. But before the two men were released from the prison, Joseph asked the cupbearer to remember him and tell Pharaoh about him. But upon his release, the cupbearer forgot and did not keep his word to Joseph. Two years later Pharaoh had dreams that no one in the kingdom could interpret. He even called on his top magicians, but they couldn't give him an answer. Then the cupbearer remembered Joseph's anointed ability to interpret dreams and told Pharaoh about him. Joseph was brought out of prison and addressed Pharaoh's need for dream interpretation.

> *And Pharaoh said to Joseph, "I have had a dream, and there*
> *is no one who can interpret it. But I have heard it said of*
> *you that you can understand a dream, to interpret it." So*
> *Joseph answered Pharaoh, saying, "**It is not in me; God***
> ***will give Pharaoh an answer of peace**."*
>
> —Genesis 41:15–16, emphasis added

What Joseph spoke were "positioning" words that addressed the main issue he had to overcome—his pride and ego. When God promotes you, and you think it's about you, you're in trouble. Joseph had finally grown and recognized from where he had received his anointing and gifts. When we see great things happening in our lives, we can either walk in pride or do what Joseph did and grow to a place where we can walk in humility, giving God the glory.

Often, positioning is not just a practical or logical thing to do. Instead, it requires a change of heart where you decide to no longer walk in pride but in humility. If any good thing has ever happened in your life, God deserves the glory for it.

As Joseph's story continues, Pharaoh shares his dream with him.

> *Then Pharaoh said to Joseph: "Behold, in my dream I stood on the bank of the river. Suddenly seven cows came up out of the river, fine looking and fat; and they fed in the meadow. Then behold, seven other cows came up after them, poor and very ugly and gaunt, such ugliness as I have never seen in all the land of Egypt. And the gaunt and ugly cows ate up the first seven, the fat cows. When they had eaten them up, no one would have known that they had eaten them, for they were just as ugly as at the beginning. So I awoke. Also I saw in my dream, and suddenly seven heads came up on one stalk, full and good. Then behold, seven heads, withered, thin, and blighted by the east wind, sprang up after them. And the thin heads devoured the seven good heads. So I told this to the magicians, but there was no one who could explain it to me."*
>
> *—Genesis 41:17–24*

If any good thing has ever happened in your life, God deserves the glory for it.

Then Joseph interpreted the meaning of Pharaoh's dream. He revealed that both dreams were actually one. The dream signified that for seven years there would be abundance in the land with a great harvest and Egypt would be richly blessed, but afterward there would be seven years of famine. In those years of famine, the loss would eat up the riches of Egypt, and Egypt would become bankrupt.

Joseph continued:

> *Now therefore, let Pharaoh select a discerning and wise man, and set him over the land of Egypt. Let Pharaoh do this, and let him appoint officers over the land, to collect one-fifth of the produce of the land of Egypt in the seven plentiful years. And let them gather all the food of those good years that are coming, and store up grain under the authority of Pharaoh, and let them keep food in the cities. Then that food shall be as a reserve for the land for the seven years of famine which shall be in the land of Egypt, that the land may not perish during the famine.*
> —*Genesis 41:33–36*

Pharaoh needed a wise man, and he didn't have to look far. Joseph was wise. Not only did he interpret Pharaoh's dream, but he also administrated the situation by offering a solution for the impending famine in Egypt. His gift not only released him from imprisonment but also continued to promote him until he became the number two leader in the known world at that time.

Think about it: When did the riches of the world come into Joseph's hands? It wasn't during the time of plenty. It was during the time of famine and poverty that he became rich. People were hungry and were coming to him for food. They were selling their farms to get enough food to live for a year. Every piece of land in Egypt came into Joseph's hands during this time.

Some of you may feel that what he did wasn't right, but if it weren't for Joseph, the people of Egypt would have starved. Not only did God use this to cause the riches of the world to come into Joseph's hands and under God's control, but He also used it to keep and preserve lives. Joseph's family members were starving in Israel and came to Egypt and bowed down before him, asking him for food—not knowing it was their brother. Joseph helped them and then revealed to them who he was, and the family was reunited.

Debt-Free

Like He did for Joseph, God has administrative insight for each of us. Not only had we, as a church, begun to manage our finances better, but my wife and I had begun to do this in our personal lives as well. We had a plan. Between 2003 and 2004, we bought ten rental houses in addition to our primary residence. Our plan was to keep them for five to ten years, sell half of them, and pay off our primary home in preparation for retirement. However, when the housing bubble hit an all-time low in 2008, the economy crashed—and our plan crashed with it. I let the pressure of what was happening in the world take away my ability and desire to be debt-free. But God continued speaking little things in our hearts, and we knew His plan for us was not dead.

We had a five- to ten-year plan to be debt-free, and we didn't owe anything on our cars or credit cards. We decided we were no longer going to take what the world was dishing out and began praying for guidance and wisdom. Even though our plan died, God's plan had not. There was still a way to be debt-free, and we prayed and believed that we would be there within ten years. We started to subdue kingdoms in the name of Jesus.

Our primary method of subduing kingdoms was to seek guidance on how to administrate properly. We began praying, asking God for wisdom, and getting in agreement with each other (Matthew 18:19). We met with counselors and spoke with our family, close friends, and people we trusted and considered wise. We also met with experts in the field of real estate, such as real estate agents, brokers, bankers, loan officers, lawyers, and insurance agents, so we could take the proper steps. We did everything we needed to do to position ourselves to walk in the promise of God.

And that promise came through. At the beginning of 2010 we bought a house and paid cash. We moved out of our old house and are currently debt-free. But it took work on our part. We gathered information, properly administrated the knowledge, and were able to subdue kingdoms. We had positioned ourselves for a tremendous breakthrough—and we received it.

Fallow Ground

Receiving God's promises doesn't come from sitting down and taking the beating the world is dishing out. If you sit there and take it, it will beat you until you have nothing and leave you as a bloody stump. But if you get on board with God's plan, He will give you the wisdom to change your situation and your life.

Contrary to the examples of David and Joseph, this verse in Proverbs states what happens when we do not administer properly:

> *Much food is in the fallow ground of the poor, and for lack of justice there is waste.*
> —*Proverbs 13:23*

This is the opposite of what we saw with David and Joseph. David administered justice, and there was plenty. Joseph administered justice, and there was plenty. Here in Proverbs, there is not proper administration, and *"there is waste."* But what does the first part of the verse say? *"Much food is in the fallow ground of the poor."* What does this mean? It means that there is an increase within the uncultivated, idle areas of our lives.

Years ago I reaped the harvest of what had been fallow ground by listening to God. I was in my office eating lunch. It was a habit of mine to get lunch, bring it back to my office, and take a break. Sometimes I would play a computer game. This particular day I was playing a game when God spoke to me. You know when you get the sense that God wants to speak to you? I had this funny feeling in my heart, and I heard God ask me, "What are you doing?"

From past experience I'd learned that usually when God asks me that question, it is because there's a problem with what I'm doing. So when He asked it, I became a little nervous.

Then He asked me, "Dan, do you know how to type?"

"You mean beyond two-finger typing? No, not really."

God then told me to get a typing program and learn how to type. For the next six weeks I took fifteen minutes from each lunch break and learned how to type—a skill that has proved invaluable to me.

Are you a good steward of your time? Are you continually positioning for breakthrough by becoming the best you that you can be? There is much increase in your fallow ground—find it.

What about your marriage? The Bible says two people become one when they get married. You and your spouse are heirs together of the grace of this life. Your marriage is one of your greatest areas of fallow ground. It is the avenue where the grace of this life flows, and the common denominator is God. You need to work on your marriage so it does not dry up. If you allow it to be, your marriage will be the most fruitful area of your life. And if you are single, trust that God will bring the right person to you. Please don't consider doing this life *"unequally yoked"* (2 Corinthians 6:14), meaning selecting a non-Christian spouse, and then expect God to bless that union. Trust Him to bring the right mate into your life.

So what happens when you don't tend your fallow ground? Years ago I knew of a mission team that went to Haiti to help a group of people. The team members took a John Deere tractor as well as other farming equipment, seed, fertilizer, pesticides, and the know-how to farm the land. They spent days teaching the local villagers how to tend their land, plant crops, and grow their own food.

The following year, the group returned to see how the people were doing and found one poor eighty-three-pound guy manually plowing the field with a hoe. The people were still starving even though they had a new tractor in the barn, along with seeds and extras—all of it was untouched and unused. They had all the materials needed for a new start; however, their mind-set had not been renewed.

While this example is literal, I'm telling you that you have fallow ground in your life from which you are not harvesting—even though God has given you all the tools to do so.

Three Questions

These three questions will tell you where you are with the administration of your life and if you are ready for breakthrough:

1. What did you do with your most recent tax refund?

2. If you received a $150,000 inheritance, what would you do with that money?

3. What are you doing with the information you've received from this book so far?

Are you taking any action? Have you taken any of the instructions in this book to further position yourself for your breakthrough? We are to walk in the light, as He is in the light. We have a responsibility once we learn something to act on it. If you didn't know you were supposed to position yourself for break-through, once you learn that, you need to respond and act.

Your answers to those three questions will tell you whether you are administrating your life correctly. Check your heart. For at least two of these questions, you should have considered sowing into a cause. This means getting involved in something you believe in, such as a charity or nonprofit, and supporting that cause. Personally, I would have tithed. You cannot subdue or expand your kingdom without properly tending its fallow ground first. Check your answers to those three questions and make adjustments. Reposition yourself today.

Prayer

Heavenly Father, thank You for whatever increase you add to my life. I pray for guidance and wisdom to properly administrate whatever You give me. I pray that You show me any fallow ground I have in my life so I can better reap my blessings. In Jesus's holy name, amen.

CHAPTER 3

THE POWER OF "SUDDENLY"

ANOTHER MAJOR ASPECT OF positioning yourself for breakthrough requires you to be proactive, not reactive. To see a breakthrough in your life, you have to get up and do something. This means you always have to be prepared, as God's timing is not our own.

> *Rise up; this matter is in your hands. We will support you, so take courage and do it.*
>
> —*Ezra 10:4, NIV*

Prepare for "Suddenly"

Several years ago, during one of our Wednesday night services, I was sitting next to Carolyn, listening to one of our other pastors preach. This was the third message in his series, and it suddenly hit me. I grabbed Carolyn's hand and told her I knew God wanted us to have this new house, and He wanted it paid in full. We grabbed hands—right there—and said, "*In the name of Jesus, we claim what God has promised for us.*" Within six weeks we closed on a short sale that would have normally taken six months. But we were prepared, and God pulled the pieces together for us.

You see, when breakthrough happens, it usually happens suddenly. However, there is a process for finding and positioning yourself for that breakthrough. One of the first steps you need to accomplish is to seek wisdom. Sometimes wisdom doesn't come instantaneously. Sometimes it takes a little while for our minds to get renewed to the plan of God.

The Bible says in James 1:5, *"If any of you lacks wisdom, let him ask of God, who gives to all liberally and without reproach, and it will be given to him."* Not only does this Scripture instruct us to ask God for wisdom, it also assures us that God will liberally give it to us. How amazing is that.

The second thing you need to do is wait for wisdom. This doesn't mean be idle, though. While waiting on God, apply yourself and work within your capacity. Do what you can in the natural while trusting that God is taking care of things in the supernatural. You are not going to receive God's best by doing nothing.

Finally, work, then test, then assess the process. If you are trying to do something, and nothing seems to be working, reevaluate your course of action to see if there's anything you need to change. Often we need to ask God to show us where we are falling short. When He reveals that to you, you need to change the process, test it again, and then reassess your results. When you achieve the desired results, all you have to do is wait on God while you keep properly administrating and directing your life. In His timing all the pieces will fall into place.

You are not going to receive God's best by doing nothing.

Use caution, however. Don't be surprised when the enemy comes for your blessing. Let's review David's situation in 1 Chronicles 14:

> Now when the Philistines heard that David had been anointed king over all Israel, all the Philistines went up to search for David. And David heard of it and went out against them. Then the Philistines went and made a raid on the Valley of Rephaim. And David inquired of God, saying,

"Shall I go up against the Philistines? Will You deliver them into my hand?"

The LORD said to him, "Go up, for I will deliver them into your hand."

So they went up to Baal Perazim, and David defeated them there. Then David said, "God has broken through my enemies by my hand like a breakthrough of water." Therefore they called the name of that place Baal Perazim. And when they left their gods there, David gave a commandment, and they were burned with fire.

> Success relies on seeking wisdom, hearing God's voice, and obeying Him.

Then the Philistines once again made a raid on the valley. Therefore David inquired again of God, and God said to him, "You shall not go up after them; circle around them, and come upon them in front of the mulberry trees. And it shall be, when you hear a sound of marching in the tops of the mulberry trees, then you shall go out to battle, for God has gone out before you to strike the camp of the Philistines."

—1 Chronicles 14:8–15

In this biblical account, David had been anointed king over Israel. He started out as king of Judah, but the people of Israel, Jerusalem, and the other ten tribes did not immediately make him their king. When they finally got on board with God's plan, they welcomed David into Jerusalem and anointed him king over all Israel.

Now, the Philistines knew that David was a hard-core warrior, but once they heard he had been anointed king, they thought maybe his plate was getting a bit full, to the point of distraction. They thought this would be the time to try and defeat him. God, however, had other plans, and David was wise enough to seek God's plan.

Do you know what happens when you get blessed, or when you start walking in breakthrough, and good things begin to happen in your life? The devil gets mad and comes instantly to steal what you have. Don't be surprised. If you're a child of God and you're getting blessed, you can expect to have some trouble.

So be aware. 1 Peter says it's important to keep your eyes open and pay attention.

> *Be sober, be vigilant; because your adversary the devil walks about like a roaring lion, seeking whom he may devour. Resist him, steadfast in the faith, knowing that the same sufferings are experienced by your brotherhood in the world.*
>
> *—1 Peter 5:8–9*

Not only do you need to pay attention, but I cannot emphasize enough how important it is for you to seek wisdom continually. Look what David did in the Chronicles passage:

> *And David inquired of God, saying, "Shall I go up against the Philistines? Will You deliver them into my hand?" The LORD said to him, "Go up, for I will deliver them into your hand."*
>
> *—1 Chronicles 14:10*

As this verse states, God is in the business of telling us what we need to hear. David was a warrior. He knew how to beat the Philistines, but he didn't go based on what he knew. He went to God with each battle to see what the plan was.

Success relies on seeking wisdom, hearing God's voice, and obeying Him. The first time David asked Him, "God, should I go up?" God told him to go. When the second battle came, David asked Him again. Often, men have an issue in this area. When we figure out how to do something, we think we've got it. We don't need the wisdom of God anymore; we'll do what we know. However, David didn't do that. He inquired again, and this time God told him not to go. Instead of going up, He told David, "Go around, come up from behind them, and when you do, you'll get the victory." David diligently sought God's advice and received wisdom and victory.

> Stay close to God—always. When we're drifting away, it's hard to hear from Him, and when it's hard to hear Him, it's hard to walk in His favor.

Like David, we need to stay close to God—always. When we're drifting away, it's hard to hear from Him, and when it's hard to hear Him, it's hard to walk in His favor.

Favor Ain't Fair

David did his part, but he couldn't do it all. When you are in God's favor, you do your part, and God will do what you are unable to do. Take a look at this testimony.

When Carolyn and I bought our current house in 2010 (with cash, remember), the refrigerator wasn't working, so we needed to buy a new one. I decided to visit a local scratch-and-dent place to see if it had anything good. Since I hadn't bought a refrigerator in twelve years, I didn't realize how expensive they had become. There was one in the store that looked as if a semitruck had hit it. Forget scratched and dented, this one looked burnt and destroyed. I asked the salesperson what it cost, and he said $700. I was shocked, and I realized that my hunt for a fridge was going to cost me a penny or two.

The salesman was walking me around and showing me the refrigerators when he stepped away to take a phone call. He came back, looked at me, and said, "You look like a pastor."

I was wearing jeans and a Denver Broncos sweatshirt. How did he know?

He said, "Somebody just called and gave you $1,163 toward a refrigerator."

"What? Is this a joke?"

"Not at all," he said. "They already paid for it. You have $1,100 for a refrigerator and $63 for delivery."

"Hallelujah! I'll take that $1,800 one right there." I said.

Here's the fun part. When I got to the counter to pay, he gave me a $100 discount. The total, including delivery, was now $1,764. I was given $1,163, which left $601 for me to pay out of pocket.

Later that week, I was closing on my house when someone from the title company asked me if I had bought a refrigerator. I told her I had.

She said, "Have you heard about the Energy Star program they have right now?"

I said I hadn't and asked her to explain.

"The government will give you a rebate on any Energy Star appliances that you buy," she said.

I figured this fridge had to be an Energy Star appliance. After all, it cost more money than my first car. Sure enough, it was. They gave me 30 percent of the original price back, which turned out to be $600. That meant that refrigerator cost me $1. Favor ain't fair.

It didn't stop there. I had to buy a new dryer, and I got a third off the price. The roof of the house needed repairing, and I got a third off that cost as well. Favor ain't fair.

We had bought our previous house five years before, and you can get a $6,500 rebate from the government if you've lived in your house for five years. People were paying me to buy this house.

We amended our 2009 tax return and got a check in the mail for one-third of the refrigerator cost, one-third of the dryer cost, and $6,500. Favor ain't fair.

What do I mean by that? Favor is not fair because it is unmerited. We do not get favor from God because we earned it or deserve it in any way. Favor is yet another gift from God—simply because He loves us.

Suddenly!

If you start doing your part—through loving and honoring God, along with being proactive with your blessings—God will do what you are unable to do. Understanding this is critical and so important. We do our part, He does His part, and suddenly there is a breakthrough in our lives.

Read the following passage from Proverbs, and pay specific attention to the word *suddenly*:

> *A worthless person, a wicked man, walks with a perverse mouth; he winks with his eyes, he shuffles his feet, he*

> *points with his fingers; perversity is in his heart, he devises evil continually, he sows discord. Therefore, his calamity shall come **suddenly; suddenly** he shall be broken without remedy.*
>
> *—Proverbs 6:12–15, emphasis added*

Suddenly can happen on both sides of the good/bad spectrum. In 2010 two of our church families adopted children from Haiti. They had been working for years to get through the adoption process, and roadblocks continually hindered the process. Then an earthquake hit Haiti. It devastated the country, but God was working in the midst of it. He made a way for those kids to arrive in Florida to loving families that had been waiting for that moment for years.

Every enemy that stood in the way of the adoption process was wiped out in that earthquake. Suddenly, all the red tape was cut into little pieces, and the children were united with their new families.

Isaiah 29 contains a perfect biblical example of this type of *suddenly*:

> *Moreover the multitude of your foes shall be like fine dust, and the multitude of the terrible ones like chaff that passes away; yes, it shall be in an instant, **suddenly**.*
>
> *—Isaiah 29:5, emphasis added*

Still, the greatest biblical usage of the word suddenly is in the book of Daniel. The prophet Daniel uses the word *suddenly* more often than any other prophet in the Bible. Here is one of those times:

And suddenly, one having the likeness of the sons of men touched my lips; then I opened my mouth and spoke, saying to him who stood before me, "My lord, because of the vision my sorrows have overwhelmed me, and I have retained no strength. For how can this servant of my lord talk with you, my lord? As for me, no strength remains in me now, nor is any breath left in me." Then again, the one having the likeness of a man touched me and strengthened me. And he said, "O man greatly beloved, fear not! Peace be to you; be strong, yes, be strong!"

—*Daniel 10:16–19*

In this instance, Daniel is saying that he is exhausted. He's given up. Then the Bible says that the angel of the Lord—or the Lord Himself—reached out and touched him, and *suddenly* a man who was weak was now strong. A man who had no peace *suddenly* had peace. A man who had no wisdom *suddenly* became wise. A man who had enemies *suddenly* had his enemies defeated.

God comes *suddenly* into the lives of His people and brings deliverance, and for that reason, you must always be ready.

Look at this verse in Malachi:

"Behold, I send My messenger, and he will prepare the way before Me. And the Lord, whom you seek, will suddenly come to His temple, even the Messenger of the covenant, in whom you delight. Behold, He is coming," says the LORD of hosts.

—*Malachi 3:1*

If you continue to position yourself, your breakthrough will come, and your enemies will no longer exist. You will have the blessing you've been looking for and the deliverance you have been seeking. But remember, you have to be proactive and do something. Keep doing what you can do, and God will do the rest. Your answer will come *suddenly*.

Prayer

Heavenly Father, thank You for loving me enough to trust me with what I've been given. Father, teach me to hear from You so that I may react proactively and always be prepared for Your timing. And Lord, teach me to respond correctly to my suddenly moments. In Jesus's holy name, amen.

CHAPTER 4

POSITION—
THEN REPOSITION

TO PROPERLY ADMINISTRATE OUR lives while expanding the kingdom outside of just church on Sundays and to be prepared since breakthrough can come *suddenly*, we need to diligently seek to obey God. Obeying God is a process that you learn with time. But God isn't looking for perfection in you; He's looking for progression. He wants you to do something. Take a step. Begin to move. If you move in the wrong direction, He will work with you, reposition you, and get you back on the right track.

Bless the Kingdom

When it comes to repositioning yourself, now is the time. You are the only one who stands in your way. Indifference will cost you. As the following scriptures say, the lazy man suffers.

If anyone will not work, neither shall he eat.
—2 Thessalonians 3:10

A lazy man buries his hand in the bowl, and will not so much as bring it to his mouth again.
—Proverbs 19:24

The lazy man does not roast what he took in hunting, but diligence is man's precious possession.
—Proverbs 12:27

Not only will indifference cost you opportunities and rewards, but wrong priorities will cost you as well. The book of Luke tells a parable of a rich man. He was so rich that he decided to build bigger barns to house all his belongings. When he built those barns, he filled them and decided to tear them down to build bigger ones. He accumulated much, but he had wrong priorities. He wasted his time focusing on building his own kingdom and accumulating wealth, rather than investing in his soul. He was aiming for his position, not God's. When God came for his soul, he hadn't properly administrated his life. His narrow-minded, greed-filled vision actually cost him his life and afterlife.

If your barns are full and you're doing very well, it's time to make blessing the kingdom a priority. You need to ask yourself this question: Because God is increasing me, what can I do to increase the kingdom? You don't want to store up only material things. Instead, get your priorities straight, get in position, and invest your blessings in someone else.

Check Your Process

A poor process, especially based on selfish priorities, will slow you down. As well, weak administration of your blessings will leave you empty. Take Moses, for example. He had numerous blessed events occur during his lifetime. God personally called him. He saw a burning bush. He had a God powerful enough to split the Red Sea. This guy was favored, anointed, and leading the children of Israel out of Egypt. But how did Moses feel about all this? He wanted to quit because his administration process was slowing him down.

And so it was, on the next day, that Moses sat to judge the people; and the people stood before Moses from morning until evening. So when Moses' father-in-law saw all that he did for the people, he said, "What is this thing that you are doing for the people? Why do you alone sit, and all the people stand before you from morning until evening?"

And Moses said to his father-in-law, "Because the people come to me to inquire of God. When they have a difficulty, they come to me, and I judge between one and another; and I make known the statutes of God and His laws."
—Exodus 18:13–16

Moses was judging every case in the camp of Israel on an individual basis. No wonder he wanted to quit. Thankfully, Jethro, his father-in-law, was a wise and godly man. He gave Moses a plan, and Moses changed his process. He brought in seventy elders to share the load, and while he still needed to administrate Israel, there was no longer a need for him to judge every single case. Are you not moving forward? Check your process, and if it isn't working, reposition and change it.

Find Him There

Before, during, and after repositioning yourself, continually seek God's guidance. The story of Elijah, in 1 Kings, is a great example of keeping God in the center of repositioning efforts. Elijah gave King Ahab a message from God that Ahab didn't like. As a result, both Ahab and his wife, Jezebel, wanted to kill Elijah. So God told him to leave—to reposition himself. Things weren't going well, and he needed to move.

> *And Elijah the Tishbite, of the inhabitants of Gilead, said*
> *to Ahab, "As the LORD God of Israel lives, before whom I*
> *stand, there shall not be dew nor rain these years, except*
> *at my word." Then the word of the LORD came to him,*
> *saying, "Get away from here."*
>
> —*1 Kings 17:1–3*

As we continue, we see that God sent provisions to Elijah during his repositioning:

> *Get away from here and turn eastward, and hide by*
> *the Brook Cherith, which flows into the Jordan. And it*
> *will be that you shall drink from the brook, and I have*
> *commanded the ravens to feed you **there**.*
>
> —*1 Kings 17:3–4, emphasis added*

What if Elijah had said, "You know what? I don't want to go *there*; I'm going to go over here instead." God did not send the ravens here. He sent the ravens to feed Elijah *there*. There is a place called *there*, and it is a place you need to find. There is wisdom from God you need to hear, and you need to move into that place to obtain it. It might be a specific hour or a location. It might be something you need to do or change—possibly your heart or mind. Regardless, it is a place where you are going to find the will of God for you, no matter what. This is repositioning. In your prayer life, ask to hear from God to assess your position and where you need to be to receive what He wants to give you.

Eventually, the brook where Elijah was staying dried up. Elijah's prophecy came true, and it did not rain for a very long time. We've all been in a similar place. We've heard from God and moved there, on His instructions. Things go well for a while, but eventually everything stops. What now? God told Elijah that he needed to go to another *there*. Read what He said:

> *Then the word of the LORD came to him, saying, "Arise, go to Zarephath, which belongs to Sidon, and dwell there. See, I have commanded a widow **there** to provide for you."*
> —*1 Kings 17:8–9, emphasis added*

Elijah obeyed. He went *there*, and God provided. You need to be willing to move and obey God. He has your provision, but sometimes you have to move *there* to get it.

Another story in the Bible reflects the importance of positioning. Elisha the prophet was building a house. One of the younger prophets was cutting down trees next to a river, and the ax-head flew off the handle and sank to the bottom of the stream. He turned to Elisha and said, *"Alas, master! For it was borrowed"* (2 Kings 6:5).

Have you ever borrowed something and then accidentally broken it? You have to buy someone a new one, and you still don't have one of your own. This was Elisha's response: *"Where did it fall?"* (2 Kings 6:6).

You may need to ask God this question. Sometimes we can become so consumed when we're walking in the blessing of God that we wander off course and then wonder where the blessing went. What happened to the goodness? What happened to the power and the anointing? Where did it fall? All you need to do is go back to where you lost it. What was the last thing God said to you? *There* is where the blessing is. Reposition yourself.

You can always go back to where you lost it. If you were to try to cut down a tree with just an ax handle, that would be hard work. There would be a lot of sweat and blisters. A little bit of bark might fly off, but that tree would remain standing, and you would be exhausted. This is, most often, the time when we look to God and say, "God, where are You?" And God will tell you, "I'm right where you left Me."

Now, some people will dispute this by saying "God will never leave you or forsake you, Pastor Dan." No, He won't leave you in an ultimate sense, but we've all lost His presence in a personal sense. Then, it was not God who left; it was you.

Potential in the Spirit

Isaiah 54 is an interesting chapter. It discusses two groups of people: those who do things in their *natural strength* and people who rely on *spiritual strength*.

> *"Sing, O barren, you who have not borne! Break forth into singing, and cry aloud, you who have not labored with child! For more are the children of the desolate than the children of the married woman," says the LORD.*
> —*Isaiah 54:1*

The words "*Sing, O barren,*" amazingly enough, refer to the spiritual people. On initial reading, it may not appear that way, but the spiritual people are the barren ones. He's speaking to people who did not naturally have children, who are barren in the natural. Let me explain.

A married woman might have four children, or even fourteen. There is a limit to the number of children a woman can have because of her natural strength. When it comes to a spiritual family, though, it is impossible to put a number on how many spiritual family members you can have. The body of Christ is worldwide, and anyone who gives his or her life to Christ becomes part of that spiritual family. I have had the privilege of speaking to thousands of people about the gospel, and many of them have given their hearts and lives to Jesus Christ. There is no natural birth process that can connect thousands of people on a family level. Our ability to produce and reproduce spiritually is much greater than our ability to produce and reproduce naturally.

We have amazing amounts of potential in the Spirit. We want to be spiritual people because we want to live to our full potential. You can only reach your full potential when living in the Spirit, not in your natural strength.

The next verse advises how to achieve that potential: *"Enlarge the place of your tent"* (Isaiah 54:2).

Notice the author isn't telling you to enlarge your tent. He's telling you to enlarge the *place* of your tent. This means conquering kingdoms by faith. If you're going to see an increase in your life, you are going to need to take more ground. Let's read on:

> *Enlarge the place of your tent, and let them stretch out the curtains of your dwellings;*
>
> *Do not spare; lengthen your cords, and strengthen your stakes.*
>
> —Isaiah 54:2

This entire passage is focusing on increase, and it has to be done spiritually. It closes in verse 3:

> *For you shall expand to the right and to the left, and your descendants will inherit the nations, and make the desolate cities inhabited.*

—*Isaiah 54:3*

Let's say you're a farmer, and you have half an acre of strawberries. If you want to grow twice as many strawberries, you need to buy another half acre. If you're a wheat farmer, and you have a thousand acres, you'll need at least another thousand acres if you want to double your crop, or yield. You have to take more ground. Enlarge the place of your tent if you want to see an increase in your life.

I was speaking with a friend once at his place of business. While we spoke, a customer walked in and asked for a particular product this company didn't sell. This was a construction company, and the product the customer sought was one needed once his project was completed.

My friend told the customer the company didn't sell that product, but, because of the nature of his business, he happened to have some on hand. My friend asked him how much the competition was charging for it. When the customer relayed the price, my friend sold the product to him, for that amount.

We began to talk about the business, and I asked, "How many times do people come in asking for that product?"

"Several times every day," he answered.

"What would happen if you started selling it?"

He said the initial investment would be approximately $2,000.

Earlier he had told me he had recently sold a piece of equipment for $9,000 and was going to use $6,000 to pay off a credit card. I suggested using the remaining $3,000 to reinvest into the business, making the field a little larger. Sell the products that connect to what you build, and customers will want you to build it. He was in absolute agreement. In faith he enlarged the place of his tent, and from that one change, his sales increased, and the business grew.

Enlarging your tent represents the law of dominion. The only things God can bless in your life are the things you bring under the authority and dominion of God. Is your family blessed? What about your home or your business? Is your sex life blessed? Any area of your life that has not come under the authority and dominion of God cannot be blessed. Some people struggle with their business because they say, "God is in charge of me on Sunday, but on Monday, I'm running that business." I have news for you: if that business doesn't come under the authority and glory of God, it will never be fully blessed.

> Any area you want to excel in must come under His dominion.

If you have a business, the first thing you need to do is develop a plan for how you are going to bless the kingdom of God through your business. If you want to see your business or family blessed, find some missionaries and support them. God will go out of His way to bless your business so those missionaries can continue to get support. You have to get your family, your business, your life under His dominion to experience His blessings in those areas. In other words, any area you want to excel in must come under His dominion.

Look!

And the LORD said to Abram, after Lot had separated from him: "Lift your eyes now and look from the place where you are—northward, southward, eastward, and westward."

—Genesis 13:14

In this verse from Genesis, what did Abram need to do? God told him that if he was going to take more ground, he had to look. Where do you have to look?

You have to look:

• Northward—Look ahead to see what's coming and where you're headed.

• Eastward and westward—Look on either side to see what's going on around you.

• Southward—Look back only to see where you've already been.

Don't let your "been through" stop your breakthrough.

Brethren, I do not count myself to have apprehended; but one thing I do, forgetting those things which are behind and reaching forward to those things which are ahead.

—Philippians 3:13

If you're going to expand your kingdom and the kingdom of God, you have to look. But why?

For all the land which you see I give to you and your descendants forever... Arise, walk in the land through its length and its width, for I give it to you.

—Genesis 13:15, 17

There are two things we can learn from Abraham: You have to look, and you have to walk it out. When you close your eyes, what do you see? How do you see yourself? Your future? What do you see yourself doing? Where are you headed? What is the will of God for you? Until you can see it, you will never experience it.

During our quest to become debt-free, Carolyn and I started asking God what He wanted for us and how He wanted us to get there. We had a lot of ideas on how we could get out of our financial mess and the failing real estate market, but when we got the idea to own our home debt-free, something clicked. Ironically, throughout the years people had repeatedly told me that I needed to be debt-free. But it did not change me because others were seeing it *for* me. If *you* see it for me, it will not change me or my mind-set. It wasn't until I saw myself debt-free that I began to make changes. You have to see it for yourself, or you will never accept the principle.

Some of you may feel as if the only thing you can perceive for yourself is failure. That's why you need to read this book. Don't let your "been through" stop your breakthrough. If you get this word deep inside of you, and let the Word of God change your thinking, you will begin to see yourself as blessed, coming in and going out (Deuteronomy 28:6). And as you begin to see yourself as more than a conqueror through Christ, who loves you (Romans 8:37), you will see positive, life-giving changes come to fruition. You'll begin to see yourself healed, well, and whole. You'll see peace in your family, full of the righteousness of God.

Abraham had to get up and look before he ever took the land God wanted him to have. Do you want to enlarge the place of your tent? Then you have to begin to see things differently.

Get your head up. Position yourself. Look around. If necessary, reposition yourself. Do everything you can to find yourself *there*—where God wants you to be—and begin to enlarge the place of your tent.

Prayer

Father God, thank You for blessing me. Help me properly administrate the blessings I receive from You. Help me not to be lazy or take any of my blessings for granted. Lord, give me the wisdom to make sure my processes are based on godly priorities and not my own. Father, I pray to hear from You so I can be *there* when You need me to be. And when I lose my direction, I pray You reposition me. I pray this in Jesus's holy name. Amen.

CHAPTER 5

POSITIONED
TO HEAR FROM GOD

WHEN YOU ARE PROPERLY administrating your life while expanding your kingdom, becoming prepared for suddenly, and repositioning yourself as needed, one of the most crucial steps is seeking heavenly guidance and wisdom for breakthrough.

Godly Wisdom

Often, God is waiting for us to make a move. The Bible says in James 4:8: *"Draw near to God and He will draw near to you."* God did a great work through Jesus Christ when He sent Him to die for your sins and mine. And I will state the following repeatedly throughout the book because I feel this point needs to be reiterated for you to truly understand its impact on your life. From God's point of view, He has already provided you with everything you need.

> *His divine power **has given** to us all things that pertain to life and godliness, through the knowledge of Him who called us by glory and virtue.*
> *—2 Peter 1:3, emphasis added*

Even though he has provided "all things that pertain to life and godliness," we still need His guidance to be successful.

I believe God does things sequentially—in a logical order—but not necessarily numerically. Say you are considering starting a new business and are still at the visionary stage when God sends a contract your way. You may get bogged down with what you think the order of things should be instead of accepting that contract and trusting God to lead you to success. Realistically, it's not as if we're trying to move God to do things for us. He's already done them. More than likely, it's God who is trying to move us to do things. You'll notice that when you finally start saying yes to God and begin to obey Him, suddenly doors start opening for other things to happen—things that were not happening before because of your lack of willingness to follow His plan. Be obedient.

Carolyn and I have had a lot of *suddenly* moments during our marriage. Carolyn once got a call from her sister who said a lawyer needed to speak with her. Now, personally, I've never had a bad call from a lawyer. Most often those work out very well for me. When Carolyn called the lawyer, he said, "I'm the lawyer representing your uncle who passed away at the beginning of March."

> From God's point of view, He has already provided you with everything you need.

Her uncle had lived a great life and had spent all his ninety years in the same small Colorado town. The lawyer said they needed to sell the uncle's house, car, and even some additional property he owned in Texas. Since he had no children, all his money had been left to his ten nieces and nephews, including Carolyn.

We didn't know we had a rich uncle. Jokingly, I used to say how great that would be, but we actually did have one. Money is certainly not everything; it's a small part of what God is doing in our lives, but it makes a big difference in what we can do for the kingdom of God. That was a wealth transfer, and God blessed us with it.

For we are His workmanship, created in Christ Jesus for good works, which God prepared beforehand that we should walk in them.

—*Ephesians 2:10*

If indeed things are sequential in the body of Christ, that verse says there are good works prepared beforehand that you should walk in them. If I am going to walk in the good works, then I need to walk to where God needs me to be.

I want to position myself for everything God has for me. We learned from Joseph how to do that. He did it through godly wisdom. We need wisdom from God because the world doesn't have the answers. Here's an example:

While working on the mortgages of the ten rental homes we had purchased, I was constantly on the phone with our mortgage company. I would get on the phone with the company at 11 o'clock in the morning and stay on the line until 2 or 3 o'clock in the afternoon. After speaking with the company dozens of times, the conversations would usually go like this:

"Are you paying your bills?"

"Yes."

"Are you behind on any of your payments?"

"No."

"Well then, sir, we cannot help you."

Wait a minute, say that again? You mean that if I am paying my bills, working hard and am a good customer, you can't help me? Are you saying I should quit paying my bills?

You see, the world doesn't have the answers.

When Carolyn and I were trying to find the will of God for our lives, we went to our bank of more than twenty years, where our daughter used to be the manager. We had quite a bit of money in our account, and we thought we'd borrow $50,000 so we could buy a $250,000 house. We both have excellent credit, so we figured there would be no problem. We were wrong. The bank denied our request.

I knew that it was the Lord's confirmation and we were not to purchase the home using the world's way. We decided not to borrow the money, which would have put us in debt. Instead, we followed the King and got on a different system. We ended up buying the house with cash. We trusted in God's economy. Answers cannot be found in the world. Trust in God for your counsel.

A Difficult Situation

Sometimes godly wisdom comes directly from God. Carolyn and I were once in a dangerous predicament. A guy came to our church in Denver, Colorado, seeking counseling. The staff scheduled him with me since I was one of the associate pastors and counseling was one of my duties. He was a youth pastor at another Denver church, whose senior pastor I knew very well. When he arrived for his appointment, he looked as if he had been beat up. He had definitely been in a fight as he had a black eye and scratches on his face. I asked him what happened.

He told me he was making the deposit of the offering money, and on his way to the bank, he was beaten and robbed. The attack was so severe he was admitted to the hospital. The church had been gracious and even took up an offering to pay for his hospital bills. But then he said to me, "You know, none of that's true."

"What do you mean?" I asked.

He said, "I lied about it all. That isn't how I got beat up. Nobody stole the offering; I spent it. I was at a gay bar when I got beat up."

Sometimes as a pastor, you hear things you wish you had never heard. It happens often, and this was one of those times.

I only have one piece of advice for people who get into difficult situations: tell the truth. It's difficult, but if you tell the truth, you generally come out clean. And that's a much better option than others finding out through someone else or by other means. Always tell the truth. I told him, "You have to go to your pastor."

After our first meeting, he came back and still hadn't told his pastor. He came back a third time, and he still had not told him. The fourth time we met was on a Tuesday, and I told him, "You've had ample time to do the right thing and come clean to your church. You need to tell your pastor before service tomorrow night because if you don't, I will."

He said, "You can't do that. You have pastoral confidentiality, and I told you this in confidence."

"It doesn't matter. I'm telling him anyway. I can no longer participate in this lie. As a pastor, you have a higher standard and calling to live up to than others," referring to 1 Timothy 3:7 and Titus 1:7–9.

Always tell the truth.

"I'll sue you," he said.

"Great," I said. "Sue away. I don't care because I'm going to do the right thing. Either you do the right thing, or I'll do the right thing. Make up your mind."

I had wrestled with his truth ever since he confessed to me. Having given him ample time to make it right, I knew I had to do something. I wasn't exactly sure what the right thing was. Since he was in a trusted position as a youth pastor and a man of great influence in the church, his deceit could be devastating to many if wrongly revealed.

He didn't do the right thing. I finally reasoned that if I were his pastor, I would want to know. In my heart there was no other option, so I told his pastors.

Afterward he went crazy. He began to follow Carolyn and me and our family. When we were at a restaurant eating, he would come in and sit at the counter or at a different table, order a cup of coffee, and watch us while we ate. When we went to the grocery store, we'd be pushing our cart down the aisle, and he would be pushing his cart the other way. Everywhere we went, he would arrive five minutes later. It was obvious he was stalking us.

The elders and senior pastor of our church encouraged us to call the police because of how serious it had gotten. When we did, they told us to file a restraining order. We did, but it didn't fix the problem. He then started harassing us in a way that he wouldn't get caught. Between midnight and 6:00 in the morning, he would drive by the front of our home, repeatedly honk the horn, rev his engine, spin the tires, and then speed away. Then he would continually call our home phone. Now, this was a time before cell phones and caller ID, and since I was a pastor, when someone called at 2:00 in the morning, I needed to answer the phone. His disturbances were a hassle, not only for us but also for our neighbors. It was an incredibly difficult situation.

> It doesn't matter how badly you think you have messed up your life—God can set you totally and completely free.

The harassment continued for several months. The police eventually tried to catch him by setting up a sting with an unmarked car at the end of our street, but he didn't come those nights, so he never got caught.

One day, at 2:00 in the morning, he was out front spinning his tires and honking the horn, waking up everybody in the neighborhood. Five or ten minutes later our phone rang. At this point, I had a desire to deal with this in the natural. The King James Version of 1 Timothy 5:22 says, *"Lay hands suddenly on no man"*; however, by that time, admittedly, I was considering laying hands suddenly and repeatedly on this guy. Thankfully I didn't take that route; I prayed for godly wisdom instead.

When the phone rang, I sat straight up in bed, and as I picked up the phone, I saw him in my spirit. God showed me where he was standing. I saw him outside the local grocery store talking on a pay phone. God showed me exactly where he was. As I spoke with him, I wrote Carolyn a note that read, "Go next door and call the police." I wrote where he was and exactly where he was standing. She got up, quickly went next door, and called the police. I intentionally kept him on the phone for several minutes longer until, at one point, I heard him sigh.

I said, "Are those cops?"

"Yeah," he said.

"God showed me where you were," I said and hung up the phone.

That had an effect on him. The wisdom of God was flowing.

He ended up spending one year in jail for violating the restraining order. Afterward he sought mental help, got better, and apologized. Part of his court order was to write us a letter of apology saying he would never bother us again. He did, and I believe he is free today.

It doesn't matter how badly you think you have messed up your life—God can set you totally and completely free. My prayers and beliefs right now are that he is doing great with God and is in ministry somewhere doing great things for God. Wisdom from God made the difference between remaining in a difficult situation and ending it.

Seeking Wisdom

Who needs wisdom from God? All of us. We've all been in a place where we've needed His help because we were facing a trial and didn't know what to do, or we needed more clarification on what to do. We got ourselves into a jam or tried to resolve it ourselves and failed. We didn't know where to turn or whom to talk to. I'm here to say that God always has the right answers, is always ready to listen to us, and is ready to help us.

I'd like to share what has been tremendously helpful to me while positioning for breakthrough. This is how I hear from God 99 percent of the time. While sometimes I hear from God directly, and it's supernatural and spectacular, most of the time it doesn't happen that way. It comes more subtly. Read James 1:2–8:

> *My brethren, count it all joy when you fall into various trials, knowing that the testing of your faith produces patience. But let patience have its perfect work, that you may be perfect and complete, lacking nothing. If any of you lacks wisdom, let him ask of God, who gives to all liberally and without reproach, and it will be given to him. But let him ask in faith, with no doubting, for he who doubts is like a wave of the sea driven and tossed by the wind. For let not that man suppose that he will receive anything from the Lord; he is a double-minded man, unstable in all his ways.*

So what is a "trial"? A trial is a test to see if you will hold on to God's promise. God has promised Carolyn and me a great marriage but not one without pressure or challenges. Whenever God promises something, the enemy comes immediately to steal it, kill it, and destroy it (John 10:10). Many of life's trials happen because we are battling for the will of God—and that battle is one worth fighting. Never give up. Never quit. Trials are the testing of your ability to hold on to what God said.

Remember Joseph's situation? He understood Pharaoh's dream, and with wisdom from God, he knew what to do with that knowledge. Like Joseph, we need to get answers and wisdom from God so we can do the right thing. Often in life, winning during the trial takes more than perseverance. Read James 1:3 again: *"knowing that the testing of your faith produces patience."*

Many of life's trials happen because we are battling for the will of God. Never give up. Never quit. Trials are the testing of your ability to hold on to what God said.

The word *patience* doesn't mean just to sit and wait; it means to endure. It's like a runner in the fifth mile of a five-mile race. His ability to press through his fatigue is exactly what patience means in this verse—enduring with strength and pushing through the trial.

When I get to heaven, I don't want to get an award for being the guy who went through the most and endured. I don't want people saying, "Look, there's Dan. He went through so much, and he's here. Praise God." I want to be like Joseph. If Joseph had been just any other guy experiencing the famine of Egypt, rather than the *guy in charge of Egypt* during the famine, we would have never even heard of him.

I want to persevere with that type of wisdom *during* the trial, not barely getting through the trial. I want to have the wisdom that allows me to overcome trials in the power of God and be able to see the will of God accomplished in my life. We need the same type of wisdom that Joseph needed.

But how do you get it? James 1:5 says, *"If any of you lacks wisdom, let him ask of God."* You have to ask for it. In a perfect world, I would give you a twelve-step plan that would give you all the wisdom you will ever need. But in reality, here is what you have to do—simple, straightforward, and to the point. If you don't know what to do, ask God for wisdom.

The verse continues, *"who gives to all liberally and without reproach, and it will be given to him."* This is a solid promise given to you by God. If you are in a situation and don't know what to do, ask God, and He will tell you.

Throughout my life God has given me wisdom in so many areas. A remarkable example of that was when I started my lawn business, I made more than a million dollars in the first five years. It all started with godly wisdom in the form of an idea—an idea that was properly administrated. Remember, when seeking wisdom, you have to be prepared to properly administrate that wisdom.

In 2010 our church had the idea to introduce a weekly Saturday night service. On the second Saturday night of each month, we have a date night, where we watch children for three hours after the service, *for free.* This is so couples can go out on a date without the expense or concern of trustworthy babysitting. Another great East Coast idea.

Pastor Dave Ellis, a former East Coast executive pastor and a graduate of Rhema Bible Training College, received a letter from Rhema asking about our latest initiatives. He shared many things with leaders at the college, but when he discussed our date night service, they were impressed. They had never heard of any church doing this before, so they published East Coast's date night initiative in their magazine, which is distributed worldwide. In a few months' time, other churches around the world followed this idea to reach out to the couples in their congregation as well as their communities. That was wisdom straight from God.

I seek wisdom regarding all personal areas of my life as well, including parenting. Point-blank and for the sake of being transparent, I don't think I know how to "father." For various reasons, sometimes kids close up and don't want your help. Also, I've learned that when I get angry or tell them to listen to me, it doesn't always work. So if I want my child's heart to open up to me, what do I need to do for that to happen?

There is usually a key, so I ask God, and He gives me the insight I need to understand what's going on in their lives. When I get that key from God, their hearts open up, and we're able to communicate openly again. By the grace of God, I have always had open communication with my children. I have been able to sit down, speak with them, and work things out. I could not be a good father without wisdom from God.

Can you think of areas in your life that could use more wisdom?

Specific Wisdom

Know that God has wisdom just for you. There is a way to decipher that, and I want to share it with you. Matthew 17 shows us that Peter once had a problem, and through personal wisdom Jesus fixed it for him.

> When they had come to Capernaum, those who received the temple tax came to Peter and said, "Does your Teacher not pay the temple tax?"
>
> —Matthew 17:24

This becomes a direct challenge for Peter. The tax collectors were questioning something Jesus had done that painted Him in a bad light. Here's a classic time in Peter's life that happens to us almost every day. Peter is feeling the fear and pressure of man come against his heart. Have you ever had that feeling?

Remember when you were in school and your teacher asked if you did your homework?

"Yeah, I did it."

"Then where is it?"

"Uhh . . . my dog ate it."

You were cornered. Your response didn't come out of truthfulness; it came out of fear and pressure. When that lie was out, you had to come up with another lie to fix it, and it all went downhill from there.

I think Peter was facing a similar situation. He didn't know the answer to the tax collector's question, and he responded with what he thought they wanted to hear. Let's continue reading:

> When they had come to Capernaum, those who received the temple tax came to Peter and said, "Does your Teacher not pay the temple tax?" He said, "Yes." And when he had come into the house, Jesus anticipated him.
>
> —Matthew 17:24–25

Now, pay attention because this is important. Jesus has already "anticipated" you—where you are right now, with whatever you're currently facing. He has "anticipated" you, and He has your answer. If God is for you, then who can be against you (Romans 8:31)? In this verse, He anticipated Peter:

"What do you think, Simon? From whom do the kings of the earth take customs or taxes, from their sons or from strangers?" Peter said to Him, "From strangers."

—*Matthew 17:25–26a*

Peter was getting nervous. He realized that Jesus knew he spoke with the tax collectors and that he gave the wrong answer. Jesus was proving that He shouldn't have to pay tax.

> Jesus has already "anticipated" you—where you are right now, with whatever you're currently facing … and He has your answer.

Jesus said to him, "Then the sons are free."

—*Matthew 17:26b*

Jesus is saying that the sons are free because He is the Son of God, sent to save them. Confused, Peter seems to be saying to Him, "You said You were going to pay this tax, and now it sounds as if You aren't going to or don't have to because You are the Son of God. Help me, Jesus; I'm in a bind here."

Jesus finished by saying, *"Nevertheless, lest we offend them"* (v. 27). Jesus didn't pay the tax for Himself or because He had to. He did it for Peter and for the people who were collecting it. This is what He said:

"Nevertheless, lest we offend them, go to the sea, cast in a hook, and take the fish that comes up first. And when you have opened its mouth, you will find a piece of money; take that and give it to them for Me and you."

—*Matthew 17:27*

That is a crazy story. I've caught a lot of fish in my day but never one that had money in its mouth. The society in which these men lived was mostly made up of shepherds, farmers, and fishermen, and they lived off the land and sea. Jesus wanted to bestow a blessing, but He needed to do it in a field that these men were familiar with and found relatable. Peter was a fisherman, which is why Jesus told him to go fishing. God knows where your "fish" are.

> God knows where your "fish" are ... You do not have a need in your life right now that Jesus has not already prepared a way to meet.

If you are searching for the blessing of God, I doubt that you will catch a fish that's full of money. When people talk about getting a big account, they call it a "big fish." God has big fish for you, and He's the only One who knows where you'll find them. He knows where that big job is. He knows where that big sale is. He knows where the big opportunity is that you need for your family. We need to continually listen so we can hear from God because He is anticipating us. You do not have a need in your life right now that Jesus has not already prepared a way to meet. Peter owed taxes, and he didn't know how he was going to pay them. He came to Jesus and was left with wisdom on how to get the money. Regardless of what you're facing, God has the right, personal wisdom just for you. And that wisdom shows you where to capture wealth.

Who Said That?

Anyone who knows God already has general wisdom because we have the mind of Christ (1 Corinthians 2:16). However, what we need beyond general wisdom is personal wisdom for specific situations. Here's how you receive that:

> *And let the peace of God rule in your hearts, to which also*
> *you were called in one body; and be thankful. Let the word*
> *of Christ dwell in you richly in all wisdom, teaching and*
> *admonishing one another in psalms and hymns and spiri-*
> *tual songs, singing with grace in your hearts to the Lord.*
> —*Colossians 3:15–16*

Here's the recipe: Get into God's Word.

Because I fill myself with the Word, I can hear from God in the spirit when I need personal wisdom for a specific situation. But normally when we do "hear" something, we ask ourselves three questions: Is that me? Is that God? Is that the devil?

Do you know how to stop doing that? Begin to tune in to the Word. When a thought enters your head, ask if it agrees with what the Bible says. If you have no understanding of the Word and haven't filled yourself with it, it will be very difficult for you to discern the will and wisdom of God. The wisdom of God is in the Word of God.

> *Let the word of Christ dwell in you richly in all wisdom.*
> —*Colossians 3:16*

Getting into God's Word doesn't mean devoting a smidgen of your time to the Word of Christ. The scripture from Colossians clearly says that the Word has to "dwell in you richly." Many people want the wisdom of God, yet they only read the Bible every two weeks. If you're searching for the wisdom of God, it is right in front of you. Pick up the Bible. It is full of God's wisdom.

Also, continue by learning to meditate on God's Word so you can properly apply God's wisdom to every aspect of your life. The more familiar and better acquainted you become with God's Word, the easier it will be for you to distinguish who said what you heard.

The Peace of God

Not only will you be able to recognize God's "voice" from meditating on His Word, but what you hear should bring you peace about your situation. Colossians 3:15 starts by saying, *"And let the peace of God rule."* Here's the whole verse:

> God's peace keeps you grounded and stable, even when everything around you is in turmoil.

And let the peace of God rule in your hearts, to which also you were called in one body; and be thankful.
—*Colossians 3:15*

First, this verse is referring to the peace of God, not the peace the world gives you. God's peace keeps you grounded and stable, even when everything around you is in turmoil.

The peace of God needs to always rule in our lives. It needs to play the constant role of an umpire. In this instance, *Strong's Concordance*, as well as several other Bible notes and commentaries, defines the word *rule* literally as "umpire." Peace is to be our "umpire." What does an umpire do? He stands behind the plate, watches the pitch, and says, "Ball" or "Strike." The umpire calls the game. Who calls the game in your heart? I can't emphasize enough that it needs to be the peace of God.

Let's say, for example, some of you single ladies are considering going out with a guy. He's asked you out, and he is handsome. You think there is absolutely no reason why you shouldn't go out with him. But deep down inside, you have a little uncomfortable feeling. There's something inside telling you not to do it. But then you tell yourself, "Yeah, but he has a nice car and goes to church and loves his mom." You try to rationalize and reason with yourself, rather than listen to your spirit, which is God saying, "Don't go there." Many emotional hurts and regrets are birthed out of not listening to God.

> Many emotional hurts and regrets are birthed out of not listening to God.

When I bought my first rental house, I had the peace of God about the purchase. I bought another one and had the peace of God about that one as well. I bought a third and still had the peace of God. Then I went to buy a fourth, and something on the inside said, "Nope, don't go there."

I ignored the disturbance of my peace and convinced myself that it was a "God decision." I tried to rationalize it by saying, "But it all worked out before." Then I walked right into a huge mess. What had I done? I had ignored the peace of God, which the Bible tells us *"surpasses all understanding."*

*And the peace of God, which passeth all understanding, shall **keep** your hearts and minds through Christ Jesus.*
—Philippians 4:7, KJV, emphasis added

According to *Strong's Concordance*, in this instance, the word keep means to "guard; to put a garrison around; or to pitch a tent of peace." You cannot go in the world's understanding of peace in any situation. Instead, you must go in the peace of God. The world tries to give you peace through secular means, such as job security and financial stability. But the peace of God keeps you stable even when all those worldly things are gone. You need to be able to follow peace. It is the umpire of your life. It's going to tell you whether something is good or bad. Let peace position you for breakthrough in your life.

Other times, peace about a decision can be verified through others, even as a group, as God uses people to give us godly wisdom and advice. But those answers are still coming from God—through others.

> *Where there is no counsel, the people fall; but in the multitude of counselors there is safety.*
> —*Proverbs 11:14*

A perfect example of this happened one particular Christmas season. In prior years, East Coast participated in the local community Christmas parade, and we would go all out. Our float held a band and people carrying banners, and we even had a separate float representing the kids in our day care. However, one year our ministry team made a decision not to participate. Several people questioned that decision because our people loved everything about the parade. They loved marching in it, watching it, and using it as a tool to witness for Christ. So many people asked what was wrong.

That was a tough question to answer. The team didn't know specifically what was "wrong." What we did know was that when we prayed about it, we could not find peace in our hearts to participate. I didn't need God to explain that to me; all I knew was we didn't have peace, so, being obedient, faithful, and trusting, we stood firm on our decision.

The only person happy about that was Scott Noy, our maintenance supervisor. Scott did a backflip off an office chair when that decision was made. Scott would have spent hours performing physical labor to build and prepare the floats, so he was thrilled when we decided to opt out that year. Many didn't share Scott's enthusiasm, however, and continued to question our stance. We stood firm, trusting what God was telling us in our hearts.

When the day of the parade arrived, it wasn't just the people of East Coast who were disappointed but most of the town. Not only was the parade canceled because of rain, but it was never rescheduled. We would have spent thousands of dollars and hundreds of employee and volunteer hours building a float that would have ended up sitting in our parking lot, unused. The peace of God ruled in our hearts and said, "Don't do it this year." Thankfully we listened.

You need to be able to follow peace. It is the umpire of your life.

Although the peace of God is strong, God obviously isn't going to call you on the phone. I am talking about inner peace. I believe this is how Jesus lived. There's a portion of Scripture where He was trying to tell us this. The Scripture never made sense to me until I saw this. Here is what it says:

> *These things I have spoken to you while being present with you. But the Helper, the Holy Spirit, whom the Father will send in My name, He will teach you all things, and bring to your remembrance all things that I said to you.*
> *—John 14:25–26*

In these verses Jesus is saying, "Look, you are going to live your life being directed by the Holy Spirit because that's how I live My life." Then He makes this amazing statement in the next verse:

Peace I leave with you, My peace I give to you; not as the world gives do I give to you. Let not your heart be troubled, neither let it be afraid.

—John 14:27

Do you know what Jesus is saying here? He's saying that the way He lived His life was by following the Holy Spirit and inner peace. In all situations, when He had peace, He followed through, and when He didn't have peace, He chose alternate paths. He was always in the right place at the right time because He followed peace.

> **Peace is a tool used by the Holy Spirit to guide us. Listen to the voice of God and follow peace.**

The good news is that He left us with that same peace. He gave us the person of the Holy Spirit to live on the inside of us. He will "bear witness" with our spirit, which means that we will "feel" the agreement of God on the inside of us, without any inner conflict or turmoil. If the situation is right, we will have peace. If the situation isn't right, we will not have peace. *Peace is a tool used by the Holy Spirit to guide us. Listen to the voice of God and follow peace.*

Prayer

Father, I thank You today for continually blessing me and giving me everything I need. Lord, as I position myself for breakthrough, I pray for wisdom to be able to define Your voice above all others. I also pray to be led by the Holy Spirit. Lastly, I pray that I have peace with the decisions I make, knowing that they are Your will. In Jesus's name I pray this. Amen.

CHAPTER 6

HOW TO CAPTURE YOUR INCREASE

AS YOU POSITION YOURSELF for breakthrough, you must learn how to capture increase. Isaiah 54 offers several principles that will help you say "Yes" to God. But equally important is knowing that once you've said "Yes," God will do whatever you can't. In the following, my trust of God's faithfulness was validated when I moved from Colorado back to Florida.

The Art of Saying Yes

Years ago, I owned a lawn and landscaping business. The work was hard, especially in the Florida heat, but while certainly not the most glamorous profession, it is a necessary one. And because of that necessity, there are thousands of landscaping businesses in Florida.

The idea for my business came to me even before my wife and I left Colorado, then the Lord told me to pursue it when we arrived in Florida. Without much detail, I obeyed the Lord but was trying to figure out exactly what He wanted me to do. Then He told me, "Just grab a lawn edger."

Back then lawn edgers weren't the stick edgers you attached to a string trimmer that today sell for ninety-nine dollars. On the contrary, they were clunky, cumbersome, and expensive pieces of equipment that were awkward to use, so most people didn't own one.

I felt as though the Lord had given me a plan, so I rented an edger for fifteen dollars for four hours. The Lord then told me to go to a street that had several houses for sale and walk up to the first one that didn't have an edged lawn. He said to do it on Saturday morning, between 8:00 a.m. and noon, when everybody would be out working on their lawns.

I went up to a house and knocked on the door. I said, "Looks like you're selling your house. You know, the number one thing that is important when selling your house is curb appeal. I can't see yours because of the grass growing over it. I will edge your grass for fifteen dollars."

"Fifteen bucks? Are you sure?"

"Yeah, I'm positive."

I got the job. As I was edging one lawn, somebody from another yard came over and asked me to do theirs. Before it was over, I had five or six yards, and I was making nearly twenty-five dollars an hour.

Soon after that, I was edging a nice elderly lady's yard, and she asked, "Do you mow?"

I didn't even own a mower at that time.

"Well, yes I do." I said. "When would you like your yard mowed?"

"Anytime you'd like."

"Okay, I'll be back later."

I went out and bought a mower that day and started mowing this lady's yard. Before I finished, I had three people approach me and ask me to mow their yards. This continued until another lady asked me if I trimmed bushes.

"Well, yes I do."

"What do you trim them with?"

"I'll be right back."

I drove to the store and bought a trimmer. I was trimming

bushes now.

A few weeks later, someone approached me and said, "I want to redo the landscaping in my backyard. Do you know somebody who does that?"

"Well, yes I do."

"Who would that be?"

"Me. I'm really busy edging, mowing, and trimming bushes in the summer, but I landscape during the winter."

By the end of that summer, I had lined up more than fifty landscaping jobs for the winter.

You see, God wants us to expand. He wants us to lengthen our cords. When I started edging, I had a plan, but I didn't have a clue that all those other opportunities would arise. Thankfully I was smart enough to say yes when they did. But more importantly, after I said yes, I stood in faith and trusted God to take care of the rest.

It is vitally important, though, that you are hearing God's direction before acting. I uprooted my family, drove 1,900 miles to a new town, and started a new career that I knew little about. And I succeeded only because I was certain that I was hearing from God. Using caution also goes for saying "Yes" to too many things, beyond a normal and balanced schedule. Remember, I kept saying "Yes" because I was starting a new business. I have known people who have exhausted themselves by taking on too much, because they felt obligated. I have even seen it in the church. Pray first about accepting responsibilities or positions, making sure they are from God, before you accept. Or you may end up finding yourself exhausted, frustrated, disappointed, and resentful.

> Reading the Bible will rewrite your vision and your future.

Four Principles for Capturing Increase

There are four principles in Isaiah 54 that will help you capture your increase.

> *Enlarge the place of your tent, and let them stretch out the curtains of your dwellings; do not spare; lengthen your cords, and strengthen your stakes.*
>
> —Isaiah 54:2

1. "Enlarge the place of your tent."

We've talked about this a bit already, but it's so important that I'm going to discuss it again. If you're going to walk in the increase that God has for you, you have to see it. For me, it was always easy to see the increase. I always said yes and dealt with any issues as they occurred. I knew I needed to buy that mower because God wouldn't open a door for me without providing a way for me to walk through it. You can work out details later on, but opportunities need to be taken when they present themselves.

What do you dream when you close your eyes? Where do you see yourself going? You may say you can't see anything but failure and obstacles. That's why we have God's Word. *Reading the Bible will rewrite your vision and your future.*

A friend once told me, "Even though my dad always said, 'You did pretty good, son,' I always knew it was never good enough." His dad was a perfectionist, so my friend lived his life thinking he was never good enough. If that's the way you think and the way you see yourself when you close your eyes, then you need to get a new picture, and it needs to come from the Word of God.

The Word tells us:

Therefore, if anyone is in Christ, he is a new creation; old things have passed away; behold, all things have become new.

— *2 Corinthians 5:17*

You are of God, little children, and have overcome them, because He who is in you is greater than he who is in the world.

— *1 John 4:4*

Jesus said to him, "If you can believe, all things are possible to him who believes."

— *Mark 9:23*

You don't have any limitations in your life other than the ones you allow and accept.

"*Enlarge the place of your tent*" is not referring to your possessions or what you have around you. It means pushing the ceiling of your personal limitations. It means expanding the boundaries of your thought processes and capabilities by seeking God, believing Him, and seeing miracles happen in your life. These actions will begin to change your life.

2. "Stretch out the curtains of your dwellings" (the law of capacities).

Stretching your curtains wide refers to properly administrating what you already have. Let's say you have half an acre of wheat, and you use a sickle to harvest it. Now imagine yourself standing on the edge of a thousand acres of wheat with a sickle in your hand. What's the first feeling you are going to experience? Overwhelming frustration right? You would experience the frustration of having the wrong tool to successfully do the job. You need a new process to capture your increase. You have to change the way you do things. You've expanded your boundaries, but you can't go into your new boundaries with the same old processes and mindsets. When you expand your borders, frequently you need to change your processes as well. I learned this when I became a landlord and owned rental properties.

Instead of doing the landlord's job, I hired somebody who knew how to do it correctly. Why? I didn't know how to be a landlord. I didn't want people looking at me and wondering how a pastor could evict them for not paying rent. I didn't want them to stumble. It's a basic principle. If they don't pay their rent, they should be evicted. If people take advantage of you and tear up your home, then they need to leave. Does that mean we do it without compassion? Of course not. That's why, being a pastor, I needed to change my process and hire a professional property manager who would achieve professional results.

Look at your life right now. Are there areas that frustrate you? Do you find yourself in situations where you're thinking, "This always gets me," "I always end up here," or "No matter how hard I try, things always work out this way"? Then it's time to change your process. If there's something in your life that turns you into a mess every time you have to contend with it, then it's time to change.

You need to constantly check your process because it's what you're using to capture the blessing of your dominion. Back when I was a single guy, I would do my laundry at the laundromat. At the time, that was the best place to meet women. It was easy for me to get a fistful of quarters and a little box of detergent. But then I got married and had four children. It's tough to do laundry for a family of six at a laundromat. It's expensive and time-consuming.

So to permanently change that process, I bought a washer and dryer. Now I had the correct process in place to do my laundry right at home. But do you ever fall behind with your laundry? Even when we have the correct process, we often fail at administration.

The same can be said with mowing your lawn. You might have a push lawn mower that's not doing the job, so you need a new process. However, if you have a riding mower, and your grass is still tall, then you're the problem. Either way, you are not administrating what you have correctly.

Ask yourself, "Do I have a process problem or an administration problem?" Are you sitting at the laundromat with a process problem, or staring at your fancy new washer and dryer surrounded by dirty laundry with an administration problem? Stretch your curtains.

> You already have everything you need to take your kingdom. God has already given us everything we need.

3. "Lengthen your cords" (the law of administration).

If you violate this law, you will have difficulty capturing your increase. Not only are your "cords" your administration, but they also anchor you to your vision. To harvest twenty thousand acres of wheat successfully (because your acres have increased), you will need combines, employees, health care, technology, transportation, sales, and so on.

Administration is a necessary process to help you capture your dominion. You already have everything you need to take your kingdom. God has already given you everything you need; put yourself in a position to receive it. How you administrate your process determines whether you will be able to capture your increase.

After Gary Keesee and I had discussed administration on our trip to Alaska, he and his wife began looking for things in their lives that they needed a new process for or they needed to administrate differently. One day he told me, "I found $1,200 the other day," and he began to tell me the story.

Gary said, "I was sitting in my office at home when a circuit blew. We had built our own home, so I knew there weren't any electrical problems. We had been there seven or eight years with no problems, but now something started blowing. I knew it had to be something that wasn't part of the main structure of the house, so my first thought was that it was something we had plugged into the wall."

They began to check the circuits when Gary noticed his five-gallon water cooler sitting in the corner. He checked it out, and sure enough, it had a short in the compressor that caused it to blow the circuit. Then he started thinking about the water cooler in general, when was the last time he'd used it? Normally when he took a break, he would go to the kitchen and get cold water from the refrigerator.

The water cooler had a hot water option on it as well that Gary realized he had never used. The water cooler had been heating water and storing it for eight years, and he had never used it.

Gary continued, "Not counting the electric bill and just counting what I paid for renting it each year, I had put $1,200 over the past eight years into that water cooler, and I had drunk from it maybe fifteen times. That's almost $100 for each glass of water. Besides that, I realized I could buy a water purification system for $120, hook it up to my existing water system, and never have to pay for a water cooler or water again."

In Gary's situation, both the process and the administration were wrong. They had bought the water cooler, stuck it in the corner, and never thought about it again.

How often does this happen to us?

For East Coast, the main problem was banking. We had been with the same bank since 1993, and we never checked to see what it was charging us in fees. We saw the bank statement every month but never thought to compare it against other banks. When we discovered the costly fees and remedied the problem by doing business with a new bank, we began to look at every area of church management. That's proper administration.

When you have a bad process in your life, as Gary did with his water cooler, it can sometimes act like a mosquito bite—you don't notice because it's just a little bump. But you might have a process in your life that's more like arterial bleeding. If so, you need to address and administrate the biggest, nastiest, most dangerous, most devastating, and most difficult things first. More often than not, however, those are the things you do not want to tackle, so you ignore them.

Take your family. If you aren't administrating your family correctly, nothing else matters—not even your business. Mark 8:36 says, *"For what will it profit a man if he gains the whole world, and loses his own soul?"* What does it profit you if you gain everything in business but lose the love and respect of your spouse and children? You have to figure out what is important in your life. Work on managing your time to put your family first.

This leads to another question: What can you delegate?

When my lawn and landscaping business began to grow, I realized I needed help. I worked by myself until I had sixty hours of work each week. Then I would hire someone and give him forty hours. Seemingly this reduced my workload by forty hours, but normally new hires were not experienced in the way I liked the work done, so I spent ten hours a week working alongside the new employee until I felt he was ready to manage the tasks by himself. This reduced my load by thirty hours.

So now I had thirty hours to dedicate to making bids, getting new accounts, promoting customer service, performing vehicle and equipment maintenance, and doing whatever else needed to be done. Then, when I got to a place where I had forty additional hours' work, I'd hire another person. This cycle continued until, at the height of my business, I had 1,200 accounts and twelve employees, divided into two crews. Though I tried, I didn't always administrate it perfectly, but when I did, it led to breakthrough, increase, and abundance. The successes were all due to proper administration.

> How you administrate your process determines whether you will be able to capture your increase.

On a grander scale, another example of a delegation opportunity can be seen in some, but not all, small churches. Their congregations remain at less than two hundred people because the pastors feel as if they have to be in contact with and touch everything and everyone in the church. If there's a problem, the pastors expect to be there. Why? It's because they like to be needed. Yet that's not the way Jesus ministered. Jesus gave ministry responsibilities to other people and had them do those tasks. The church body can take care of itself if its people love, minister to, and care for one another. That's how Jesus was able to minister to tens of thousands of people. Again, that's proper administration.

If you don't give some of your responsibilities away, you will never experience increase in your life. I can hear some business owners saying, "But they can't do it the way I can." Who cares? Recognize that nobody is going to do it as well as you think you can. If you don't let it go, you're going to be bound to doing it yourself forever.

The same principle applies to churches. If the only gospel ever heard consisted of sermons, and only on Sunday mornings, then we would be severely limiting our influence and ability to touch lives. It's the same principle. Lengthening your cords by delegating is an important part of proper administration and is imperative to your success.

Be careful, however, and stay aware once you've reassigned a task to someone else. If you notice a dip in quality and production, you must equip through the dip. This means that as a manager you continue to lend proper tools and give training to those persons until they reach the appropriate level of expertise.

4. "Strengthen your stakes" (the law of fortitude).

Fortitude means "mental and emotional strength in facing difficulty, adversity, danger, or temptation."[1] When you step out into your vision or calling, all hell can break loose. You might even call this the "law of pressure." You have to dig deep into the vision of what God has called you to do, and if you are not resisted in any area of your life, then you are not pursuing the calling of God. If you are called and anointed and reaching others, the enemy will hate you, seek to destroy you, and pull the rug out from under you every chance he gets. You need to be anchored to what God has called you to do.

As for the problem Carolyn and I had, we started out saying we wanted to be debt-free, but we realized our stakes weren't as strong as we needed them to be. We had a ten-year plan. We were going to buy ten houses and rent them out. After the renters had paid rent for ten years, we were going to sell our rentals, pay off our house, and own a couple of rental houses free and clear. It was a good plan, but we made a mistake. We married ourselves to the process, and you can't be so sternly committed to a process that you won't allow for flexibility.

When the housing market began to fail, we held on and didn't change anything. Then it was at the point where we couldn't sell any of our houses. The meltdown of the real estate market was unlike anything anyone had ever seen. By staying married to the process, it about drained us financially, which naturally led to our being emotionally and mentally drained as well. Instead, we should have been married to the vision. The vision was to be debt-free, and regardless of what happened to the market, the vision didn't change.

If you position yourself, this will be a year of miraculous breakthrough. God wants you to own houses and land debt-free. Is that your vision? Strengthen your stakes and anchor yourself to it. Fortify your stakes by driving them deep because the wind is going to blow. The devil is going to try to rip off that area where you have taken dominion. The only thing that is going to keep you anchored is you being firmly rooted in the will of God.

What did Carolyn and I do? We changed the process. We downsized, sold our house, and moved. When we initially bought that house, we were convinced it was our retirement home, but that process broke down, and we had to get rid of it. That house is now gone, but that isn't important. The important thing is for you to listen to and obey what God has called you to do.

Ask yourself these questions: Where have I compromised on the vision? Where have I given up or shut down because of pressure? When I realized that Carolyn and I had given up, the first thing I did was pray and ask God to change my heart. This is what I prayed:

God, change my heart. Don't let my experience be my future. Don't let what I have experienced in these past two years in the housing market paint the only picture I have in my heart and mind for my future.

Don't let the jobs you've lost or the businesses that have failed paint the picture of who you are. You are not disqualified; you are merely resisted. Stay resilient. Strengthen and fortify your stakes.

"Do Not Spare."

This part of Isaiah 54:2 relates to all four of those principles I just mentioned:
- Do not spare—"Enlarge the place of your tent."
- Do not spare—"And let them stretch out the curtains of your dwellings."
- Do not spare—"Lengthen your cords."
- Do not spare—"And strengthen your stakes."

Notice I mentioned "Do not spare" in every aspect of this scripture. "Do not spare" means that you better get busy! It means for you to give it all you have and not hold back in any capacity. Do not hold back on, or *do not spare*, your time, energy, efficiency, talent, effort, willingness, obedience, and so on. You fill in the blank. Get busy, and always give it your very best.

Four Questions

Ask yourself the following questions. Couples, sit down with your spouse or significant other and answer the questions, first as individuals, then as a couple. Singles, your answers will be between you and God.

1. What do you see when you close your eyes?

2. What frustrates you about your life?

3. What are your time and money producing?

4. Where have you given up or shut down because of pressure?

After you answer each of those questions, ask God for wisdom. Ask Him to make clear to you where you lost track of the vision; then ask Him to reveal your next steps. He will direct them. The Bible says in Psalm 119:105, "*Your word is a lamp to my feet and a light to my path.*"

As of 2019, Carolyn and I own our home and one of our rental houses outright. Our overall plan is to own two more rental homes so that they become a steady income for our retirement years. Even though we had to change the process, I'm still not giving up on everything we had and lost in the real estate market. The Bible says this in Proverbs:

> People do not despise a thief if he steals to satisfy himself when he is starving. Yet when he is found, he must restore sevenfold; he may have to give up all the substance of his house.
>
> —*Proverbs 6:30–31*

We are going to get our money back. Our goal was to own rental houses plus our own, and we are further along today than when we began this process. Now we are on the right track, and nothing will stop us until we have completed the vision God has set before us.

Prayer

Heavenly Father, I thank You for loving me. Let me be quick to say yes when You call me. Let me stand strong in faith and be without doubt of Your faithfulness. Lord, help me see my increase by enlarging the place of my tent, stretching my curtains, lengthening my cords, and strengthening my stakes—all the while, Lord, never sparing my resources. In Jesus's name, amen.

CHAPTER 7

BOLDLY TAKE
YOUR BREAKTHROUGH

"Sing, O barren, you who have not borne! Break forth into singing, and cry aloud, you who have not labored with child! For more are the children of the desolate than the children of the married woman," says the LORD. "Enlarge the place of your tent, and let them stretch out the curtains of your dwellings; do not spare; lengthen your cords, and strengthen your stakes. For you shall expand to the right and to the left, and your descendants will inherit the nations, and make the desolate cities inhabited. Do not fear, for you will not be ashamed; neither be disgraced, for you will not be put to shame; for you will forget the shame of your youth, and will not remember the reproach of your widowhood anymore."

—Isaiah 54:1–4

THE BIBLE IS PEPPERED with words and events that instruct us to take action. Isaiah 54 unwaveringly emphasizes the importance of taking control of your situation: "*Enlarge* the place of *your* tent. . . *lengthen your* cords . . . *strengthen your* stakes." Nowhere does it state to wait around passively for something to happen for you. That is not God's way.

Desperate Measures

In a more extreme example, Genesis 38 gives us a situation requiring excessive boldness, stemming from desperation. In this divine "do-over," the main characters are Judah and Tamar. Judah is one of the twelve sons of Jacob, and those twelve sons make up the twelve tribes of Israel. Judah is also the tribe that our Lord is from. Jesus is the Lion of the tribe of Judah.

Judah had three sons, and his eldest, Er, married a young girl named Tamar. But Er's life with Tamar did not please the Lord, and Scripture says the Lord killed him. Back in those days, when a married male in the family died, the culture required the next brother in line to marry the widow and raise up an heir to maintain the family lineage. These rules were in place so the nation of Israel did not get wiped off the map before it ever got started. At that time, there were only about seventy people in the "nation." So Er's brother, Onan, took Tamar as his wife. But Onan never planted his seed in her either so she could produce an heir, so God killed him too.

While I will not elaborate too much on God's wrath, as that is not the subject of this book, I will thank God for Jesus and that judgment has fallen on Him for the sins of the world. We no longer live in fear of not pleasing God. Jesus died in mankind's place, and that is great news for us. If you still do not know Him, revisit Chapter 2 and receive your gift of salvation so you can take your place in the kingdom.

At that point, Judah, Tamar's father-in-law, requested that she move back into her own father's home while he raised up his young son, Shelah. Judah promised Tamar that she could marry Shelah when he turned of age.

*Then Judah said to Tamar his daughter-in-law, "Remain a
widow in your father's house till my son Shelah is grown."
For he said, "Lest he also die like his brothers." And Tamar
went and dwelt in her father's house.*

—Genesis 38:11

For years Tamar waited patiently at her father's home, but
nothing happened. She was in waiting with no results. Her life was
empty, and she was alone.

During that time, Judah's wife died, and at some point
he decided to travel to Timnah to join his workers during
sheepshearing season. Tamar learned of his trip and decided to
take action because she had become frustrated with Judah's lies
and deceit.

Tamar knew he would be traveling through the town of
Timnah and would most likely be drunk from the celebration of
wine and sheepshearing. So Tamar disguised herself as a prostitute, as revealed in Genesis 38:12–14.

*Now in the process of time the daughter of Shua, Judah's
wife, died; and Judah was comforted, and went up to his
sheepshearers at Timnah, he and his friend Hirah the
Adullamite. And it was told Tamar, saying, "Look, your
father-in-law is going up to Timnah to shear his sheep."
So she took off her widow's garments, covered herself with
a veil and wrapped herself, and sat in an open place which
was on the way to Timnah; for she saw that Shelah was
grown, and she was not given to him as a wife.*

Verse 12 starts, *"Now in the process of time,"* and we can tell
some time had passed. Shelah was now an adult: *"for she saw that*

Shelah was grown, and she was not given to him as a wife." And even though we do not know exactly how much time had gone by, her father-in-law's intentions—or lack thereof—were clear to her since years had passed.

What do you do when you can see that something is not going to go your way? When something that is supposed to happen— something you have a right to by inheritance—doesn't?

She had married into a wealthy and influential family and was entitled to the family inheritance. Specifically, because Tamar had married the firstborn son, she knew that she and her family were now heirs to her husband's wealth. (Remember that this family grew to become Christ's royal lineage.)

> We need to use life's pressures to launch us forward, not stop us.

Tamar didn't lose her hunger, nor did she give up and give in. She was not going to settle for barrenness.

Biblical events are used to teach us valuable life lessons. Some of these, namely the ones of spiritual perseverance, encourage us to imitate the actions in the story, as is the case with the Good Samaritan. However, I cannot find a lot of practical help from the example of Tamar when it is received verbatim since these are not practical instructions. In this case, we should learn from it, not imitate it. All strangeness aside, when I see the spiritual ramifications of the actions taken, I receive great insight into how to boldly reach for a breakthrough.

Your Inheritance As a Christian

You are an heir to the throne—you have rights to your inheritance, your covenant.

*. . . and if children, then heirs—heirs of God and joint
heirs with Christ, if indeed we suffer with Him, that we
may also be glorified together.*

—Romans 8:17

Are you waiting for:
• Your marriage to improve?
• Your children's salvation?
• Healing you were promised?
• Successful business ventures?
• Walking in the favor of God?
• Prosperity—being debt-free?

2 Corinthians 1:20 tells us, *"For no matter how many promises
God has made, they are 'Yes' in Christ. And so through him the 'Amen'
is spoken by us to the glory of God"* (NIV).

What do you do when you are not receiving what you have
been promised from God's Word? Do you complain or confess?
Do you grieve or believe? Do you give up or get up?

*So she took off her widow's garments, covered herself with
a veil and wrapped herself, and sat in an open place which
was on the way to Timnah; for she saw that Shelah was
grown, and she was not given to him as a wife.*

—Genesis 38:14

Do you wear the garments of passivity and settle for what life
hands you? Or do you rise up and put on the garments of action?
Again, I am not suggesting that her actions should be imitated,
but I am saying that in God's kingdom, you have a spiritual inheritance that satan will try to take from you every day.

I see two types of people and churches in this story. The first are people, and churches, that, when pushed back, stay back and let the obstacles stop them.

Then some people and churches, when pushed back, become even more determined to capture their inheritance. That godly determination launches them forward.

Think of reaching for what is rightfully yours as a slingshot or a bow. Not only are these both weapons, but they are also projectile weapons. The slingshot's band is designed to be stretched to its most tense capacity, then released to fire a projectile at the greatest speed possible. And the further a bow's string is stressed backward, the more fiercely it launches the arrow forward. These tools work best when under considerable strain and pressure. Similarly, we need to use life's pressures to launch us forward, not stop us.

You cannot let yourself get ripped off from your inheritance as you sit down and take the abuse. You must fight for what the enemy is stealing from you. Jesus suffered greatly to purchase your inheritance. Fight for it.

Again, consider the literal and figurative lessons here. This does not apply to the natural because there is a danger associated with this type of behavior. Don't fight with your relatives about money. Your spiritual battles are not against man.

> *For we do not wrestle against flesh and blood, but against principalities, against powers, against the rulers of the darkness of this age, against spiritual hosts of wickedness in the heavenly places.*
>
> *—Ephesians 6:12*

Be Bold

Assuredly, I say to you, among those born of women there has not risen one greater than John the Baptist; but he who is least in the kingdom of heaven is greater than he. And from the days of John the Baptist until now the kingdom of heaven suffers violence, and the violent take it by force.

—*Matthew 11:11–12*

"*The violent take it by force.*" What does that mean? It means the people of God rising up and fighting for what is theirs. We must apprehend what we were apprehended for. Don't weakly reach for the promises of God. Firmly reach for them, and then take them with boldness.

Not as though I had already attained, either were already perfect: but I follow after, if that I may apprehend that for which also I am apprehended of Christ Jesus.

—*Philippians 3:12, KJV*

This verse tells us to lay hold of what God has laid hold of us for. We have to reach for what God has designed us for.

Regardless of her circumstances, Tamar was willing to fight for her inheritance. The death of Er did not stop her. The deceit of Onan didn't stop her. Even the rejection by Judah didn't stop her. Even though she was deterred, she remained determined. Don't lose your determination.

Let's read on in Genesis 38.

So she took off her widow's garments, covered herself with a veil and wrapped herself, and sat in an open place which was on the way to Timnah; for she saw that Shelah was grown, and she was not given to him as a wife. When Judah saw her, he thought she was a harlot, because she had covered her face. Then he turned to her by the way, and said, "Please let me come in to you"; for he did not know that she was his daughter-in-law. So she said, "What will you give me, that you may come in to me?" And he said, "I will send a young goat from the flock." So she said, "Will you give me a pledge till you send it?" Then he said, "What pledge shall I give you?" So she said, "Your signet and cord, and your staff that is in your hand." Then he gave them to her, and went in to her, and she conceived by him. So she arose and went away, and laid aside her veil and put on the garments of her widowhood.

—Genesis 38:14–19

This Is a Wild Story.

Tamar refused to be barren, and considering all the elements needed to achieve this goal, you can understand her tenacity.

What kind of person will you be? What kind of church will we be?

What are you refusing to settle for? Will you mope and moan, or will you do whatever is necessary to move beyond "barrenness?" Will you do whatever you have to in order to receive all the promises of God?

Please do not misunderstand me—I am in no way advocating illicit sex or trapping someone with a pregnancy. We are looking past the physical here and focusing on who we are to be as spiritual beings —bold, confident, and willing to fight for what God has given us.

So now Tamar's pregnant with the promise. You see, she was the firstborn's bride, which meant that she was heir to the family fortune. Yet Judah continually tried to strip that away from her, so she fought back.

In the story, Judah sent a goat to pay for his indiscretion with "the harlot" (Tamar), but she could not be located; they could not find her. Don't ever settle for just the payment of a goat when you can have the throne.

> **Don't lose your determination.**

Later the Bible says:

> *And it came to pass, about three months after, that Judah was told, saying, "Tamar your daughter-in-law has played the harlot; furthermore she is with child by harlotry." So Judah said, "Bring her out and let her be burned."*
>
> *—Genesis 38:24*

What? So not only was Judah ripping off his lineage by deceiving Tamar, but now he was negatively judgmental, self-righteous, and unmerciful. He wanted to burn her alive. I suspect his mindset was one of relief to finally be able to get rid of her. Maybe he even thought, "My good name has been tarnished, but now my problem is solved. I do not have to give her to my son; I have an out."

The next verse says:

> *When she was brought out, she sent to her father-in-law, saying, "By the man to whom these belong, I am with*

child." And she said, "Please determine whose these are—
the signet and cord, and staff."

—Genesis 38:25

She saved herself from being burned alive by producing the covenant symbols that Judah had given her in Timnah. Those symbols reflected her rightful place in the family. As a Christian, you stand on the name of Jesus, the blood of the covenant, and the Word of God.

So Judah acknowledged them and said, "She has been
more righteous than I, because I did not give her to Shelah
my son." And he never knew her again.

—Genesis 38:26

This last part means that Judah was never intimate with Tamar again, but the story does not end there.

Now it came to pass, at the time for giving birth, that
*behold, **twins** were in her womb. And so it was, when she*
*was giving birth, that the **one put out his hand**; and the*
midwife took a scarlet thread and bound it on his hand,
saying, "This one came out first." Then it happened, as he
drew back his hand, that his brother came out unexpect-
*edly; and she said, "**How did you break through?** This*
breach be upon you." Therefore his name was called Perez.
Afterward his brother came out who had the scarlet
thread on his hand. And his name was called Zerah.

—Genesis 38:27–30, emphasis added

Tamar gave birth to twins named Perez and Zerah. Perez

means breakthrough, while Zerah means light. And even the birth symbolically represents two people or two churches. One lamely puts out his hand, expecting to receive, while the other one suddenly breaks through, ahead of his brother, and reaches out for the prize. One settled for penetrating his obstacle, whereas the other did not settle for less than a total breakthrough.

Declare this:

- "We are passive with people—we do not need to *steal* their blessings.
- We are pleased with God—we rest in what He has done.
- We aggressively pursue His promises.
- We attack the problem.
- We pulverize the perpetrator. We possess powerful praise as we boldly reach for our breakthrough."

Following are other great examples, from the New Testament, of people who boldly reached for their breakthrough.

In this example, we see that the paralyzed man solicited the help of his friends to get down through the roof.

Now it happened on a certain day, as He was teaching, that there were Pharisees and teachers of the law sitting by, who had come out of every town of Galilee, Judea, and Jerusalem. And the power of the Lord was present to heal them. Then behold, men brought on a bed a man who was paralyzed, whom they sought to bring in and lay before Him. And when they could not find how they might bring him in, because of the crowd, they went up on the housetop and let him down with his bed through the tiling into the midst before Jesus. When He saw their faith, He said to him, "Man, your sins are forgiven you."

—Luke 5:17–20

And here we read about the bold persistence of a Syrophoenician woman who sought healing for her daughter.

Then Jesus went out from there and departed to the region of Tyre and Sidon. And behold, a woman of Canaan came from that region and cried out to Him, saying, "Have mercy on me, O Lord, Son of David. My daughter is severely demon-possessed." But He answered her not a word. And His disciples came and urged Him, saying, "Send her away, for she cries out after us." But He answered and said, "I was not sent except to the lost sheep of the house of Israel." Then she came and worshiped Him, saying, "Lord, help me." But He answered and said, "It is not good to take the children's bread and throw it to the little dogs." And she said, "Yes, Lord, yet even the little dogs eat the crumbs which fall from their masters' table." Then Jesus answered and said to her, "O woman, great is your faith. Let it be to you as you desire." And her daughter was healed from that very hour.

—Matthew 15:21–28

In the following scripture a woman who suffered with an issue of blood for twelve years boldly pressed through the crowd to touch Jesus.

And suddenly, a woman who had a flow of blood for twelve years came from behind and touched the hem of His garment. For she said to herself, "If only I may touch His garment, I shall be made well." But Jesus turned around, and when He saw her, He said, "Be of good cheer, daughter; your faith has made you well." And the woman was made well from that hour.

—Matthew 9:20–22

Again, we see how Jesus reacts to persistence in this example of the two blind men who determinedly followed Him and would not shut up.

When Jesus departed from there, two blind men followed Him, crying out and saying, "Son of David, have mercy on us." And when He had come into the house, the blind men came to Him. And Jesus said to them, "Do you believe that I am able to do this?" They said to Him, "Yes, Lord." Then He touched their eyes, saying, "According to your faith let it be to you." And their eyes were opened.

—Matthew 9:27–30

So the questions are:
- What type of Christian will you be?
- What kind of church will we be?

As for me and my house, we are boldly going for our breakthrough.

Prayer

Lord, thank You for creating me for a purpose. Let me be bold while seeking You and Your promises. And whenever I feel defeated, give me the strength to never give up; give me the strength to proceed, move forward with confidence, and accomplish what You designed me for. In the mighty name of Jesus, amen.

CHAPTER 8
YOUR TURN

IN 2010, I LEARNED the benefits of positioning for breakthrough through a series of changes my church had gone through to be more responsible with what God had given us. Later, while on vacation in Alaska, I learned how important it was to share those "positioning for breakthrough" principles.

Then, through the course of a year, I had shared my processes with at least a half dozen people. Time and time again, I saw the positive things the principles had done in their lives, in addition to my personal successes. I now realize that God was continually placing me in situations where I could share the information with others. That's when I decided to share it on a grander scale in hopes of helping many more people.

And like the people these principles have already helped, I am sure you have a different opinion of what *breakthrough* is. I think everyone's definition will be different, based on his or her most pressing needs. However, one thing remains the same—breakthroughs improve our lives and move us closer to our next stage of spiritual growth.

You can practice these principles during any stage of your life, whether unmarried or married thirty years, pre-ministry or already ordained, just starting a family or a parent of four. Every facet of your life can be improved by using the principles in this book.

Application

This knowledge works best when you break down certain areas

of your life and apply the principles individually over each area. Take *family*, for example. It helps to break it down even further: husband and wife, kids, finances, vacation, income streams, retirement, and so on. For ministry, perhaps the breakdown could be visitors/guests, finances, communication, and follow-up, to name a few. These instructions are best if applied to individual tasks instead of trying to apply them all under one large, overwhelming category. Tackle the specific issues that need to change within each situation.

If you want to be debt-free, the first challenge would be to assess where you are financially; make changes, no matter how small (e.g., make your own coffee instead of buying gourmet coffees, pack your lunches for work rather than buying lunch, rent movies rather than going to the theater); and then become a better steward of what you have. I discussed proper administration in Chapter 1. If you want to succeed, make an effort and find an organized system that works best for you.

There are no "magic" fixes in life. Positioning for breakthrough requires work on your part. And by work I mean making changes in your life, mostly behavioral. Every chapter of this book gives you instructions on how to move in that direction and shares a series of life-changing assessments and advancements, with each one bringing you closer to reaching your goals.

What If Nothing Happens?

So what happens if nothing happens? What if you follow the steps and still have an unfulfilling, stagnant life with no breakthrough? It might be time to reassess where you are spiritually. Do you have any unforgiveness in your heart? Do you have ill will toward anyone? Are you practicing an intentional, secret sin that has allowed a door to open for satan?

It is important that you recognize satan's role in your setbacks. Be assured he is not here to make your life better or easier, especially if you are seeking a God-focused goal. He is your enemy with only one clear goal in mind, as seen in John 10:10:

> *The thief does not come except to steal, and to kill, and to destroy. I have come that they may have life, and that they may have it more abundantly.*

But good news is stated in the latter part of that scripture. Jesus is here to make our lives better.

So when things aren't working out for you, be bold and ask God to reveal any bondage in your life that may be impeding your progress. When revealed, the oppression needs to be removed. You may need to confess something hidden or repent from current behavior. You may need to forgive someone who has wronged you. Or you may even need to forgive yourself. Regardless of what it is, you need to address the conflict immediately. You may want to seek prayer from a trusted spiritual leader.

> What distinguishes Christians from non-Christians is how we manage life when it becomes derailed.

What If Problems Arise?

Living the Christian life doesn't mean the rest of your days will be spent floating on a glory cloud with everything going your way. Most likely it's the opposite. As I stated, satan is not your friend, so expect to meet opposition and conflict. Circumstances will come up during your positioning efforts. However, what distinguishes Christians from non-Christians is how we manage life when it becomes derailed.

As Christians, we live in the hope of God and know that He is always—and will always be—with us. We know that we can give God all our problems, and although those problems may seem big, they will never be bigger than Jesus. And by knowing this, we need never live in fear because God is for us, and He is greater than any adversary we can imagine.

> *Have I not commanded you? Be strong and of good courage; do not be afraid, nor be dismayed, for the LORD your God is with you wherever you go.*
> —*Joshua 1:9*

> *Even though I walk through the valley of the shadow of death, I fear no evil, for You are with me; Your rod and Your staff, they comfort me."*
> —*Psalm 23:4, NASB*

> *What then shall we say to these things? If God is for us, who can be against us?*
> —*Romans 8:31*

Do not give up. Do not stop moving forward.

Nothing or no one is greater than our God. That alone should bring us all the comfort and confidence we need to succeed in our efforts.

So no matter how things look in the natural, do not give up. Stick with it. God is handling your issues in the supernatural. He wants you to enjoy the journey you are taking to receive His best for you. He doesn't want you distracted with worry or fear. Do not stop moving forward.

Receive Your Breakthrough

I wrote this book because of how these truths helped Carolyn and me, and I wanted to share them with everyone who is stale or dry or stuck in his or her life. It's also for those who really want to get ahead and grow in all areas of their lives. Now it's your turn. You have some work to do.

I pray that the ups and downs of my life and the wisdom and knowledge I gained from them encourage you to experience incredible breakthrough.

Stay focused, do as instructed, and prepare to receive your God-focused breakthrough.

> *So David went to Baal-perazim and defeated the Philistines there. "The LORD did it." David exclaimed. "He burst through my enemies like a raging flood." So he named that place Baal-perazim (which means "the Lord who bursts through").*
>
> —*2 Samuel 5:20, NLT*

Prayer

Heavenly Father, I thank You for loving me so much that You want me to prosper in all areas of my life. I thank You for freely giving me the wisdom to understand and apply the principles in this book. Please show me any areas of weakness that need to be removed so as not to impede my progress. I pray that Your continued love and guidance flows as I commit to making changes toward my desired God-focused breakthrough(s), regardless of obstacles that may arise. Thank You for being with me always and keeping the enemy at bay. I love You, Lord. In Jesus's name I pray this. Amen.

FROM THE DESK OF PASTOR DAN STALLBAUM

WHILE I DILIGENTLY WORKED on this book, our church experienced some of the most altering transitions to date. Had I known what was to come, I would have thought it improbable to seamlessly manage these changes. I've listed some of the biggest changes here:

1. The retirement of two senior, executive pastors and their wives, who also held prominent positions in the church

2. The addition of Pastor Matthew Stallbaum as co-pastor of East Coast Christian Center

3. The complete transformation of our university, East Coast Christian University (eccuequipped.com), including a new provost

4. The complete transformation of our children's ministry

5. The complete transformation of our finance department

6. The installation of a new Cocoa campus pastor

7. The installation of a new Merritt Island Avenue Worship Center pastor

8. The installation of a new youth pastor

9. The complete restructuring of the cleaning staff

10. The complete restructuring of the maintenance staff

11. The installation of a new office staff manager

12. The installation of a new administrative staff

13. The installation of a new Merritt Island Parkway campus administrator

14. The restructuring of our morning radio show, Morning Breath (eccc.us/morningbreath), including the complete rearrangement of the host/guest host rosters

15. The purchase of a radio station

16. The creation of a new online ministry platform (soon to be released)

17. The purchase of five acres to build a permanent location for our currently portable Viera, Florida campus.

Most of these changes were unforeseeable. Yet now that they are in place, they have positioned our church for years of upcoming growth and spiritual success. And because it has become second nature for East Coast to position itself for future breakthroughs, all these transitions happened without even the slightest break in our services, functionality, or duty as community spiritual leaders.

The work was hard behind the scenes but not unmanageable. We were able to achieve the changes successfully and move forward toward breakthroughs. As it would happen, God had given me the words "transition that leads to transformation" for the church for 2017, and was He right.

The words God had given me for 2018 were "transformation that leads to action," and that proved to be prophetically accurate as well, as many transformed their lives to be where God wanted them to be.

In 2019, as we progress into more of God's glory, I'm inspired to think that more people will take their next step. What is your next step with Jesus? I pray you always position yourself for the riches He has for you.

After you read this book and begin following its practices, you, too, can be prepared for transformation that leads to your breakthrough.

May God continue to bless you richly.

—PASTOR DAN STALLBAUM

Positioning for Breakthrough – End of Chapter Prayers

Prayer 1

Heavenly Father, thank You for all of my blessings, gifts, and assets. Lord, I ask for wisdom to properly administrate what You have already given me. Father, I ask You to show me how to make changes that better benefit Your kingdom. I ask for Your help to conquer my weaknesses, so I no longer have to fight the same battles over and over. Lord, I want positive results and changes in my life. I want to be victorious and prepared for when my breakthrough comes. In Jesus's name I pray this. Amen!

Prayer 2

Heavenly Father, thank You for whatever increase you add to my life. I pray for guidance and wisdom to properly administrate whatever You give me. I pray that You show me any fallow ground I have in my life so I can better reap my blessings. In Jesus's holy name, amen.

Prayer 3

Heavenly Father, thank You for loving me enough to trust me with what I've been given. Father teach me to hear from You so that I may react proactively and always be prepared for Your timing. And Lord, teach me to respond correctly to my suddenly moments. In Jesus's holy name, amen.

Prayer 4

Father God, thank You for blessing me. Help me properly administrate the blessings I receive from You. Help me not to be lazy or take any of my blessings for granted. Lord, give me the wisdom to make sure my processes are based on godly priorities and not my own. Father, I pray to hear from You so I can be *there* when You need me to be. And when I lose my direction, I pray You reposition me. I pray this in Jesus's holy name. Amen.

Prayer 5

Father, I thank You today for continually blessing me and giving me everything I need. Lord, as I position myself for breakthrough, I pray for wisdom to be able to define Your voice above all others. I also pray to be led by the Holy Spirit. Lastly, I pray that I have peace with the decisions I make, knowing that they are Your will. In Jesus's name I pray this. Amen!

Prayer 6

Heavenly Father, I thank You for loving me. Let me be quick to say yes when You call me. Let me stand strong in faith and be without doubt of Your faithfulness. Lord, help me see my increase by enlarging the place of my tent, stretching my curtains, lengthening my cords, and strengthening my stakes—all the while, Lord, never sparing my resources. In Jesus's name, amen.

Prayer 7

Lord, thank You for creating me for a purpose. Let me be bold while seeking You and Your promises. And whenever I feel defeated, give me the strength to never give up; give me the strength to proceed, move forward with confidence, and accomplish what You designed me for! In the mighty name of Jesus, amen.

Prayer 8

Heavenly Father, I thank You for loving me so much that You want me to prosper in all areas of my life. I thank You for freely giving me the wisdom to understand and apply the principles in this book. Please show me any areas of weakness that need to be removed so as not to impede my progress. I pray that Your continued love and guidance flows as I commit to making changes toward my desired God-focused breakthrough(s), regardless of obstacles that may arise. Thank You for being with me always and keeping the enemy at bay. I love You, Lord. In Jesus's name I pray this. Amen.

NOTES

Chapter 1

Proper Administration: The Missing Link

1. "Tracing Quotations," Quote Investigator, accessed February 23, 2019, quoteinvestigator.com/2017/03/23/same

2. Melissa Chan, "Here's How Winning the Lottery Makes You Miserable," Time, January 12, 2016, time.com/4176128/powerball-jackpot-lottery-winners

3. Bible Hub, s.v. "work," accessed December 5, 2018, biblehub.com/greek/2038.htm.

4. Dictionary.com, s.v. "legalism," accessed December 5, 2018, dictionary.com/browse/legalism.

Chapter 6

How to Capture Your Increase

1. Dictionary.com, s.v. "fortitude," accessed December 20, 2018, dictionary.com/browse/fortitude?s=t.

POSITIONING FOR BREAKTHROUGH: GOD'S PLAN FOR YOUR VICTORY

danstallbaum.com

WE WOULD LIKE TO HEAR FROM YOU!

If this book helped you achieve a breakthrough, we would love to hear your story and pray in agreement with you! Through a testimony, or any other input, please consider sharing how this book impacted your life.

The best way to connect with us is by email at info@danstallbaum.com, phone, 321-452-1060, or via Facebook.com/pastordanstallbaum.

IF YOU'RE A FAN OF THIS BOOK, WOULD YOU CONSIDER SHARING IT WITH OTHERS?

There are several ways you can help me get the word out about the message of this book...

- Post a review on Amazon.

- Write about the book on your social media.

- Recommend the book to friends— word-of-mouth is still the most effective form of advertising.

- Consider purchasing additional copies as gifts.

You can order these books from wherever you purchase your favorite books, including

WANT TO KNOW MORE?

If you would like more information about East Coast Christian Center (eccc.us) in Brevard County, Florida, you can contact us:

670 North Courtenay Pkwy
Merritt Island, FL, 32953
321-452-1060

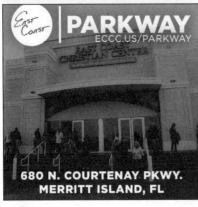

EAST COAST CHRISTIAN UNIVERSITY (ECCU)

East Coast Christian University is building believers; training them to effectively utilize the tools God gave them. No matter your age, stage of life, or background, ECCU is the place for you to discover your life purpose and grow your relationship and understanding of God and His Word.

670 North Courtenay Pkwy
Merritt Island, FL, 32953
321-452-1060

eccuequipped.com

A DRIVE-TIME DEVOTIONAL TO JUMP-START YOUR DAY

All Scripture is God-breathed and is useful for teaching, rebuking, correcting and training in righteousness.
-2 Timothy 3:16, New International Version

Decades ago, Pastor Dan started his own, daily devotional program by reading a Bible chapter each morning. He realized the power that starting his day in God's word – first thing – gave him and he wanted to share that practice with others. *Morning Breath*, East Coast's radio show, was born based on that premise.

Listeners are encouraged to read from a publicly available, prescribed Bible chapter list. Then, Pastor Dan and a guest host, discuss the chapter live on air, bringing insight to God's word.

Morning Breath airs each weekday at 5:00am, 7:30am and 4:00pm, EST, on WMIE 91.5 FM (heard locally along the east coast of Central Florida).

In addition, you can download the *Morning Breath* FREE PODCAST, at: eccc.us/morningbreath. Also go to the website to request the free Bible Chapter reading list or call 321-452-1060.

MORNING BREATH

DRIVE TIME RADIO SHOW

NEED A COACH ON CHURCH DYNAMICS AND LEADERSHIP?

Pastor Dan Stallbaum works with church leaders to create strategies that will help them better lead and serve their communities. If you are looking for someone with hands-on experience in the trenches of church ministry and leadership and who has the skills and wisdom to be a trustworthy mentor and coach, contact Pastor Dan at:

Facebook.com/pastordanstallbaum
or info@danstallbaum.com